D0726891

EDWARD BOND

MICHAEL MANGAN

Northcote House
in association with the
British Council

1 2 APR 2005

1217487

© Copyright 1998 by Michael Mangan

First published in 1998 by Northcote House Publishers Ltd, Plymbridge House, Estover Road, Plymouth PL6 7PY, United Kingdom.
Tel: +44 (01752) 202368 Fax: +44 (01752) 202330.

All rights reserved. No part of this work may be reproduced or stored in an information retrieval system (other than short extracts for the purposes of review) without the express permission of the Publishers given in writing.

British Library Cataloguing-in-Publication Data
A catalogue record for this book is available from the British Library

ISBN 0-7463-0883-3

Typeset by PDQ Typesetting, Newcastle-under-Lyme
Printed and bound in the United Kingdom

3 APR 2006

Contents

Acknowledgements   vi

Biographical Outline   vii

Abbreviations and References   ix

Introduction   1

1   From the Early Plays to *The Sea*   4

2   Questions and Answers   33

3   Towards Postmodernism   65

4   Conclusions?   95

Notes   100

Select Bibliography   103

Index   106

Acknowledgements

I would like to thank the friends, students and colleagues with whom, over the years, I have taught, discussed, staged and been to see the plays discussed here. In particular I would like to acknowledge with thanks the assistance and feedback I have received from students and staff in Loughborough University English and Drama Department, and its Postgraduate Theory Reading Group, who heard and responded vigorously to an early draft of some of the ideas here. Conversations with John Bull, Richard Boon and members of Big Brum TIE company were more helpful than they probably thought at the time, while I owe special thanks to Philip Roberts and Zara Mangan for their help and suggestions and attention to detail. My biggest debt of gratitude is to Edward Bond himself, whose correspondence and co-operation were invaluable in the preparation of this study. Acknowledgements are also due to the publishers of his work and of other copyright material. Any errors of fact, taste, logic or interpretation are, of course, the sole responsibility of the author.

Biographical Outline

1934   Born in Holloway, London.
1940   Evacuated, first to Cornwall, then to East Anglia.
1945–9 Educated at Crouch End Secondary Modern School.
1953–5 National Service. Begins to write short stories and plays.
1958   Working in a factory. Invited to join Royal Court Writers' Group, for which he becomes a regular playreader.
1962   *The Pope's Wedding* performed, Royal Court Theatre.
1965   *Saved* performed, Royal Court. Bond becomes a full-time writer.
1966   Royal Court successfully prosecuted under the Theatres Act 1843 for performing *Saved* without a licence. Bond Oscar-nominated for *Blow-Up.*
1968   *Early Morning* performed, Royal Court. *Narrow Road* performed, Belgrade Theatre, Coventry.
1969   Edward Bond Season at Royal Court.
1971   *Lear* performed, Royal Court.
1973   *The Sea* performed, Royal Court. *Bingo* performed, Northcott Theatre, Exeter.
1975   *The Fool* performed, Royal Court. Receives *Plays and Players* Award for Best Play (1976).
1976   *The Swing* performed, Almost Free Theatre.
1977   Northern Arts Literary Fellow at Universities of Newcastle and Durham. Honorary Doctorate, Yale University.
1978   *The Bundle* performed, RSC Warehouse Theatre. *The Woman*, directed by Bond, is the first new play to be performed on the National Theatre's Olivier stage.
1979   *The Worlds* performed by Newcastle University Theatre Society, and subsequently by Activists Youth Theatre

	Club, Royal Court. Both directed by Bond.
1980	South Bank Show (LWT) dedicated to Bond's work. Bond involved in defence of Brenton's *Romans in Britain*.
1981	*Restoration* performed, Royal Court Theatre, directed by Bond.
1982	*Summer* performed on National's Cottesloe stage, directed by Bond. Theatre Writer in Residence, University of Essex.
1983	*Derek* performed, RSC Other Place. Visiting Professor, University of Palermo.
1985	*War Plays* trilogy performed, RSC Barbican.
1986	*Human Cannon* performed, Quantum Theatre, Manchester.
1989	*Jackets* performed, Lancaster University and Haymarket Theatre, Leicester.
1992	*In the Company of Men* premièred in France, Centre Dramatique Nationale de Savoie.
1993	Two television plays broadcast: *Olly's Prison* and (for BBC Schools) *Tuesday*.
1995	*At the Inland Sea* performed, Big Brum TIE Company.
1996	*In the Company of Men* performed, RSC Barbican. Directed by Bond. *Coffee* performed, Rational Theatre, Glamorgan (subsequently restaged at Royal Court 1997).

Abbreviations and References

AA   *A-A-America* and *Stone* (London: Methuen, 1976)

AIS   *At the Inland Sea* (London: Methuen, 1997)

C.   *Coffee* (London: Methuen, 1995)

DCAA   *Derek and Choruses from After the Assassinations* (London: Methuen, 1983)

L1   Ian Stuart (ed.), *Edward Bond Letters I* (Luxembourg: Harwood, 1994)

L2   Ian Stuart (ed.), *Edward Bond Letters II* (Luxembourg: Harwood, 1995)

L3   Ian Stuart (ed.), *Edward Bond Letters III* (Luxembourg: Harwood, 1996)

OP   *Olly's Prison* (London: Methuen, 1993)

P.   *Poems 1978–85* (London: Methuen, 1987)

P1   *Plays One: Saved, Early Morning, The Pope's Wedding* (London: Methuen, 1977)

P2   *Plays Two: Lear, The Sea, Narrow Road to the Deep North, Black Mass, Passion* (London: Methuen, 1978)

P3   *Plays Three: Bingo, The Fool, The Woman, Stone* (London: Methuen, 1987)

P4   *Plays Four: The Worlds, The Activists' Papers, Restoration, Summer* (London: Methuen, 1992)

P5   *Plays Five: Human Cannon, The Bundle, Jackets, In the Company of Men* (London: Methuen, 1996)

T.   *Tuesday* (London: Methuen, 1993)

TPMP   *Two Post-Modern Plays: Jackets and In The Company of Men, with September* (London: Methuen, 1990)

WP   *The War Plays* (London: Methuen, 1991)

Introduction

I may be a good or bad writer, but I am an innovative one (*L2* 84)

In a much-quoted letter, written in 1977, Edward Bond said

> When I first started to write plays I thought my life's work would be
> the span of plays that began with *The Pope's Wedding* and in fact
> ended with *The Sea*. But when I'd finished these plays I found, of
> course, that there were many other plays I wanted to write. I next
> wrote three plays (*Bingo*, *The Fool* and *The Woman*) in which I tried to
> deal with society at three important stages of cultural develop-
> ment... That series of plays is now finished.[1]

When Simon Trussler wrote the monograph on Edward Bond
which appeared in the previous series of Writers and their
Work, Bond had only just moved beyond that first 'span of
plays'. Trussler was writing in the early seventies, by which time
Bond was already recognized as a dramatist of major importance,
and the last play which he includes is *Bingo* (1976). This current
volume aims to update the story, to suggest how far Bond has
come, and on what roads, since he discovered that *The Sea* was
not, after all, the end of his life's work. Bond's career as a theatre
writer now encompasses a period of about forty years, from his
earliest apprentice pieces to the present day, and an essential
feature of that career has been Bond's continual theatrical
experimentation.

This experimentation has been of two kinds. On the one hand
there is a great diversity of technique from one of Bond's plays
to the next. Bond's theatre covers a wide range of styles, genres
and settings. He moves from working-class social realism to
surrealist comedy, from the large-scale epic to the tightly
controlled, intimate drama of family life. He writes plays with
contemporary settings, futuristic settings, period settings, and

1

fantasy settings. He embraces and subverts mythic structures, and he writes boardroom dramas about the workings of the business world. Equally importantly, though, within any given play it is possible to see the same inquiring, exploratory mind at work. With each new style or genre which he inhabits, he does so with a sense of exploring it, of testing its limits, often of quarrelling with it. His dramaturgy is essentially a critical one: he seems continually to be looking at ways of critiquing, expanding or opening up the conventions which he inherits.

But if one aspect of Bond's work involves constant change, innovation and experiment, another involves constancy and continuity. Throughout the course of his writings there have been certain themes, certain ideas and beliefs about the world which have remained essentially unchanged. Asked in a recent interview about how he felt he had changed since his earliest plays, Bond replied

> My basic message remains the same, but it has developed. If you want to live in an inhuman world and accept it you become inhuman. You need to say why that world is inhuman, why it matters to you, and why you want to change it. It all relates to ownership. What I aim at is a form of socialism in which people can own themselves.[2]

In what follows I shall be looking at individual plays, but also suggesting some of the broader movements in terms of which Bond's work might be understood, and trying to indicate how these continuities and changes, styles and ideas, form a pattern throughout his work. Bond himself, as we have seen, is sensitive to the idea of such patterns, and has often described his work in terms of chronological series or cycles of plays. Taking this cue from Bond, this study will take a broadly chronological (rather than thematic or theory-led) approach, and will cover Bond's dramatic output from his earliest publicly staged plays up to his most recent work. Although I will look at most of Bond's published or performed plays to date, I shall not attempt to deal with them all in equal detail; it is not feasible in a work this size. Instead I will focus on some key texts – and on some key moments within texts – which I take to be paradigmatic of Bond's dramaturgy.

I will also be making use of Bond's own non-dramatic writings about the theatre, politics and his own works. Bond is well known for the amount of commentary on his own writing which he has published. There are newspaper articles, numerous interviews in a wide variety of journals, and prefaces, notes, postscripts and commentaries are published with many of his plays. In addition there is currently in the process of publication, a series of volumes of Edward Bond's letters, selected and edited by Ian Stuart, which is an invaluable resource for anyone interested in Bond's work. These writings, however, do not constitute any magical answers to the difficulties which Bond's plays often raise. They are not repositories of simple truths about 'what the plays really mean', and anyone looking for this in them will almost certainly go away disappointed and probably more confused than before. Bond's polemical essays should be considered – the same way as his directing of his own plays should be considered – not as attempts to tie down the meanings of his plays, but as further explorations in themselves of the questions and issues which the plays raise.

1

From the Early Plays to *The Sea*

In all my plays there are always two worlds ... And my plays exploit
the difference between the two worlds, taking the character from
one world to the other.[1]

EARLY WORK

The first series of plays is the one about which there is the least
to say. Between 1957 and 1961, when he began work on *The
Pope's Wedding*, Bond wrote about fifteen plays for radio, stage
and television. Little is known about any of them except for their
titles: they include *The Tragedy*, *Silo's New Ruins* and *The
Performance* (radio plays); *The Broken Shepherdess* (a play for
television) and stage plays *A Woman Weeping*, *The Asses of Kish*,
and *Klaxon in Atreus' Palace*, and some of the plays and fragments
which were later written for the Royal Court Theatre Writers'
Group. None of these early works are now available for reading
or performance; like many mature artists, Bond is somewhat
embarrassed by his juvenilia, which he describes as being 'well-
meaning and incompetent – totally incompetent. And rather
embarrassing to read, I should think'.[2] While there is nothing to
be said about these individual playtexts, there is a point to be
made about the general nature of Bond's period of apprenticeship: that it was spent writing plays in isolation, sending them
off for consideration, and having most of them rejected and
returned. This is, perhaps, the classic, almost archetypal,
experience of the young writer, whether poet, novelist or
playwright. It is, however, in contrast to the experience of the
later radical playwrights who, in the sixties, followed Bond into

4

the cultural limelight and with whom he is often associated. Writers such as Howard Brenton and David Hare and many of their contemporaries and successors learned their craft in a very different way. Their earliest works were often written and performed at university (Bond was largely self-educated), after which they formed small touring companies to perform their plays, or else had their work put on in London fringe theatres. Theirs was, in short, a communal, collaborative and essentially theatrical apprenticeship, taking place in the rehearsal room as much as at the typewriter. These playwrights were frequently writing directly for companies and actors known personally to them, whom they could expect to stage their work – and, indeed, much of these writers' earliest work, good or bad, did get staged. They learned their craft, and made their mistakes, in public. Bond's apprenticeship, by comparison, was a more conventionally literary one – even when, in 1958, he joined the Royal Court Writers' Group. For him the advantages may have lain in the longer incubation period during which he could concentrate on his craft as a writer. It also meant that Bond was never a 'fringe' writer in his early days – largely because the fringe, as it developed during the late sixties and early seventies, hardly existed when Bond began to write plays. Club performances at the Royal Court Theatre fulfilled some of the functions of such a fringe, perhaps, but the widespread network of small-scale venues which later nurtured so many voices of the alternative theatre was non-existent.

THE POPE'S WEDDING AND SAVED

It was on the strength of one of these early works, *Klaxon in Atreus' Palace*, which Bond submitted to the Royal Court Theatre, that he was invited to join the Royal Court's Writers' Group. He submitted a couple of short plays to the Group, 'one of which', according to director William Gaskill, 'was rather Beckett-like, and the other rather Brecht-like in style'.[3] In 1962 *The Pope's Wedding*, his first full-length play to be staged, was performed at the Royal Court, in a production without décor. This is the point at which he began the phase of his work which he describes above, comprising 'the span of plays which began with *The Pope's Wedding* and in fact ended with *The Sea*'.

The Pope's Wedding is set in a contemporary working-class community, although, unlike most theatrical portrayals of working-class life at the time, it deals with an agricultural environment rather than an urban industrial one. The action takes place in a deeply rural community in an Essex backwater somewhere near Saffron Walden, a community where agricultural workers still carry scythes, and whose local economy is still dependent on the land and in touch with the changing seasons. Bond's own parents had come from such an East Anglian community, and during the war Bond himself had been evacuated to his grandparents' home near Ely. But *The Pope's Wedding* is not a pastoral play, nor is it a Weskerian meditation on a return to rural roots. When asked why he had set the play in such a location, Bond replied, 'I didn't have a car and it was the nearest really rural area I could get to...it's near London but it's really very rural'.[4] The community exists at the point where two worlds meet – 'traditional' rural society which is beginning to feel the impact of late twentieth-century industrialism. *The Pope's Wedding* is the first of many plays by Bond which are set, either literally or metaphorically, between two worlds.

It tells the story of a young man, Scopey, his courtship and marriage to his girlfriend Pat, and the way in which that disintegrates as he becomes obsessed with the elderly recluse, Alen. Scopey is convinced that Alen has some special knowledge or understanding. He is disappointed, however, and finally, in a spate of irrational violence, he murders the old man. The title refers to 'an impossible ceremony – Scopey's asking for an invitation for something that isn't going to happen, that *can't* happen'.[5]

The first production of *The Pope's Wedding* received mixed but predominantly friendly reviews. Bernard Levin enthused that 'this bizarre and unclassifiable piece is an astonishing *tour de force* for a first play, and if it comes to that, would be an astonishing tour de force if it were a fifty-first...Mr. Bond is an original. We shall hear more of him'.[6] (*Daily Mail*, 10 December 1962). On the other hand, an anonymous reviewer in the *Observer* complained that, among other things, the play was 'too elliptical',[7] initiating a long tradition of reviews which condemn Bond's work for being 'difficult', 'oblique' or 'obscure'.

Part of the difficulty which *The Pope's Wedding* presented to its original audience is that it looks at first as if it is quite simply a

6

naturalistic play – and therefore to be understood only in terms of the questions we usually ask of naturalism. The stage world created by naturalistic theatre asks an audience to accept it as a fully realized image of the real world. It encourages the audience to view this world (through the absent fourth wall) and to judge its inhabitants according to the 'common-sense' criteria of the dominant value system, to ask questions about them as individuals, and as the play progresses to understand them more and more as fully rounded human beings. From their outward behaviour, words and appearance the audience is asked to deduce their inner emotional and intellectual life, and it is towards the laying bare of this that the drama works. What naturalistic theatre, typically, does *not* do is question the everyday 'common-sense' values themselves.

The early scenes of *The Pope's Wedding* seem to establish it as a naturalistic text. The dialogue appears to conform in most respects to the style of working-class social realism which had been embraced by the Royal Court in the late fifties and early sixties. The play opens, for example, with a none-too-serious scuffle between two of the village lads:

> BILL *forces* SCOPEY's *head under his left armpit.* SCOPEY *is bent double from the waist.*
> SCOPEY. Lego. Lemeegoo!
> BILL. 'Ow's that for an arse, boy?
> *He hits* SCOPEY's *arse with his right hand.* SCOPEY *hits him in the kidneys with his right fist.*
> Ow! Bastard.
> SCOPEY. I 'ope that'll teach yoo a lesson.
> BILL. Bastard!
> SCOPEY. Next time yoo keep yoor 'ands a yoorself.

> (P1 229)

As the play develops, however, we find that its apparent naturalism is gradually (the effect is a subtle one) compromised or undercut. The narrative becomes increasingly episodic and fragmented, and towards the end of the play it becomes clear that many of the answers which naturalism usually affords to the questions of the drama are not, after all, going to be provided. The usual logic of naturalistic character, for example, which focuses upon clarity of motivation and consistency of action, becomes secondary in *The Pope's Wedding*. The nature of

Scopey's obsession and the reasons for his final act of violence are never fully explained to the audience, who are left with more questions than answers about what leads him to do what he does.

In the play's first production the anti-naturalistic elements of the text were emphasized by the style of the production. This was in part a practical and pragmatic matter, having to do with the conditions under which *The Pope's Wedding* was first performed, and for which it was first written. It was presented as a Sunday night members-only performance at the Royal Court on 9 December 1962, in a production directed by Keith Johnstone. The Sunday night events, by their very nature, could not offer an illusionistic set: scenery and costumes were kept to a minimum, and what little of these there were were usually borrowed from stock or cannibalized from plays already in production, rather than being specially made to fit the needs of the play itself. In fact, by a wonderful irony, this production of *The Pope's Wedding* was presented on a set which had been fashioned out of the left-over bits and pieces from recent performances from the Court's production of Samuel Beckett's *Happy Days*. The juxtaposition of dialogue based on sharply observed everyday reality with the scenic bric-à-brac of existential absurdism seems a fertile start to Bond's career as a playwright – and Alen, indeed, could almost come out of a play by Beckett or early Pinter. But even more potent is the image of Bond arriving in the landscape of one of the classic writers of the modern theatre, and taking it over and using it for his own, utterly different, purposes.

Bond's own note makes it clear that the style of that first production is to be followed in subsequent stagings of the play.

> The stage is dark and bare to the wings and back. Places are indicated by a few objects and these objects are described in the text. The objects are very real, but there must be no attempt to create the illusion of a 'real' scene. In the later scenes the stage may be lighter and Scene Fifteen may be played in bright light.   (*P1* 227)

For a writer with a commitment to naturalistic theatre the lack of costume or set might simply have been a nuisance which had to be lived with; the audience might be asked to imagine what the set would be like in a 'proper' production. For Bond, however, this was not the case: the minimalist setting was very much in tune with his exploratory approach to theatre, in which naturalism was to be a starting point rather than a destination. The social and physical environment in *The Pope's Wedding* is indicated through metonym and symbol rather than through iconic representation. For example, in scene 2 of the play the countryside is invoked by the placing of a single apple on the stage. In itself there is nothing radical in this small detail, of course – theatre has always made use of metonymy, whereby the part is made to stand for or suggest the whole (think of the Elizabethan stage). Nonetheless, it indicates that the relationships between what the audience actually *sees* and the meanings which they are to deduce from them are not always going to be straightforward.

A corollary to this scenic approach to the stage is the way in which Bond is also beginning to experiment with point of view in the play. In a later interview he talks about the way in which he wanted the recluse, Alen, to appear in the early scenes to be 'more sombre and more as he appeared in Scopey's imagination rather than the tetchy man he was... [in the early scenes] he should be rather enigmatic'.[8] By doing this he makes the audience see things from Scopey's point of view, and concentrates the audience's sense of Scopey's own search for understanding. Scopey becomes the eyes through which the audience see Alen – and the world.

It is a technique which becomes shocking at the end of the play, when the character to whom the audience feels closest unexpectedly turns into a killer for reasons which the audience may not entirely understand. Scopey (the name implies 'looking', or 'seeing') is convinced that Alen holds some important secret, that he has some wisdom which he, Scopey, desperately wants to share. It is his disappointment in this search which leads to the final act of violence against the old man. Bond links his own, and the audience's search for meaning with that of Scopey:

> The important thing is not to be intrigued or puzzled by images but always to understand them. So that what I wanted to do was to try and get inside the image, and see what it was all about. That is what Scopey does in the play, and in the end he kills a man and wears his clothes in order to find out. And of course, there's nothing there. The

truth about this man's charisma, you see, is that it's based on nothing.[9]

Thus the naturalism which had seemed, in the fifties and sixties, to be the obvious theatrical language with which to articulate working-class experience, is already under pressure, even in this, the most naturalistic of Bond's plays. There is already under way a search for a more complex stage language, one which has its roots in naturalism, but which is also beginning to open out more symbolic areas of meaning on the stage, and asking different kinds of questions. A completely naturalistic play would be asking, and answering, certain kinds of questions about Scopey's culminating act of violence: what motivated him to do it? what were his feelings for Alen at such and such a point? was there a homoerotic attraction between the two men? was Scopey acting out an Oedipal pattern? These are not irrelevant questions: *The Pope's Wedding*, after all, uses a naturalistic vocabulary for much of the time. However, they are not the most important ones. By refusing to provide simple answers to them, Bond's play leaves a gap in the audience's experience of the play. It also opens up another, wider question: 'what does it *mean* that Scopey kills Alen?'

In fact Scopey is the first in a long line of central Bondian protagonists who are searching for something, and who themselves become lost. In later plays this 'something' which is being sought will become clearly defined. In *The Pope's Wedding*, though, Scopey's search is less sharply focused. His interest in Alen starts in curiosity, and moves through various degrees of intimacy and urgency as Scopey cares for the old man who becomes a father-figure to him; it ends, though, in a dead end of disappointment and violence.

On the strength of *The Pope's Wedding* a new play was commissioned by the Royal Court, and it was this which really brought Bond to the attention of the theatre-going public. The public outcry over *Saved* (1966), and some of the legal consequences of that outcry, constitutes one of the landmarks of contemporary British theatre history.

The first production of *Saved* was directed by William Gaskill – once more on a minimalist set, and once more, technically, as a private 'club' performance, staged for members of the English Stage Company at the Royal Court. This time, though, the private nature of the performance was an attempt to protect the play and the theatre from prosecution. In 1966 theatre in the UK still operated under the provisions of the 1843 Theatres Act, which bestowed on the Lord Chamberlain's office the function of acting as the official censor of all publicly staged theatrical events. The Lord Chamberlain's office had read *Saved* and demanded a large number of cuts and changes to it. These Bond had refused to make, and so the decision was made to present *Saved* as a private, club performance. Neither the official censors nor the press critics took this technicality seriously, however, and the Lord Chamberlain's office charged the theatre with presenting the play without a licence, while the press, getting wind of something controversial, also treated the production as if it were a major public run. The reviews were widespread – and almost entirely condemnatory. Irving Wardle's review in *The Times* is not untypical:

> The most charitable interpretation of the play would be as a counterblast to theatrical fashion, stripping off the glamour to show that cruelty *is* disgusting and that domestic naturalism *is* boring. But the writing itself, with its self-admiring jokes and gloating approach to moments of brutality and erotic humiliation, does not support this view. In so far as the claustrophobically appropriate action has any larger repercussions, it amounts to a systematic degradation of the human animal.[10]

The intensity of loathing which the play – or, in some cases, merely the reports of the play – provoked may be shown by the following anecdote. One newspaper critic who wrote a review praising *Saved* was the *Observer*'s Penelope Gilliatt, one of the few perceptive enough to see that 'this isn't a brutish play. It is a play about brutishness, which is something quite different.' She received a torrent of angry and indeed violent correspondence for her temerity in daring to defend the play. 'Two people sent torn-up programmes. One enclosed a newspaper photograph of my child with her head cut off and daubed with red ink'.[11] The violence portrayed in *Saved* is matched by the violence of the outcry against it.

Saved shows a clear stylistic and thematic progression from *The Pope's Wedding*. Once again, a 'boy-meets-girl-boy-loses-girl' story acts as a framework for something darker and more violent. The play deals with the relationship between a young

11

couple, Len and Pam. First seen as young lovers in the early scenes of the play, the relationship between them soon cools as Pam is drawn to one of Len's mates, Fred. Len and Pam end up living together, in Pam's parent's house; the joyless, loveless relationship between Pam's mother and father looks set to be repeated in the younger generation, as Pam treats Len with increasing indifference, and eventually with contempt. This early part of the play deals with the emotional effects of social deprivation, but it is also fast-moving and witty, with many moments of high energy, comedy and laughter. Once more, the story is told in episodic form, with the audience being invited to fill in narrative gaps between scenes. One of these episodes, however, took the play into new territory. Whereas the moment of unexpected violence in *The Pope's Wedding* comes at the end, with Scopey's murderous attack on the old man, in *Saved* it comes halfway through the play and involves a famously shocking stage image.

Scene 6 starts apparently peacefully: Len and Fred are fishing in a park. Pam now has a baby, which she claims is Fred's, while Len well-meaningly continues – despite her obvious indifference to him – to attempt to hold their relationship together. There is little animosity between the two young men, although Fred tends to patronize Len. When they are joined both by a group of Fred's mates, and also by Pam – doped up with tranquillizers, unable to cope with parenthood or her own failing relationship with Fred – the scene turns more bitter. After arguing with the uncaring Fred, Pam runs off, leaving the baby in the pram on the stage. Fred and his mates (Len at this point has run off after Pam) begin to play with the pram, a game which becomes increasingly violent as they continue.

> BARRY. What about the nipper?
> PETE. Too young for me.
> *He 'touches' Barry.*
> BARRY. 'Ere! Dirty bastard!
> *He projects the pram viciously after Colin. It hits Pete.*
> PETE. Bastard! . . .
> *Pete pushes the pram viciously at Barry. He catches it straight on the flat of his boot and sends it back with the utmost ferocity. Pete sidesteps. Colin stops it.*
>
> (P1 74)

Eventually it turns deadly. The boys start tormenting the child, spitting at it, then throwing things at the pram – burning matches and stones. The baby is killed.

Part of the scene's effect derives from the casualness of the violence. As the boys treat the baby with increasing aggression, there is an unnerving combination of carelessness and cruelty.

> *[Barry] spits*
> MIKE. Got it!
> PETE. Give it a punch.
> IKE. Yeh less!
> COLIN. There's no-one about!
>   *Pete punches it.*
>   Ugh! mind yer don't 'urt it.
> MIKE. Yer can't.
> BARRY. Not at that age.
> MIKE. Course yer can't, no feelin's.
> PETE. Like animals.

(P1 77)

It is sometimes suggested that the violence in this scene is 'ritualistic', and certainly there is a carefully crafted shape to the scene, in which the aggression builds up slowly towards its climax. But to talk about ritual misses out the firm grounding in realism which the scene possesses. Its power comes from a pattern which arises out of ordinary, even innocent, exchanges between the boys. They tell themselves that their actions are, effectively, victimless. Colin encourages Pete to punch the child and then, extraordinarily, shows 'concern' that Pete should not hurt it in the process. The baby, the lads explain to each other, cannot feel – it is not fully human. In this way they distance themselves from the full horror of what they are doing, and in their own minds they turn it back into something blameless, mundane. For the audience, however, watching this inexorable escalation of violence building slowly towards the death of the child, no such distancing is possible.

The responses which *Saved* elicited from audiences and critics are well documented. In fact, audience response, in its more general sense, is a crucial issue in understanding the workings of Bond's plays: from the beginning his drama has been concerned not merely with putting certain events, incidents, characters and ideas on stage, but with the effect that these

13

would have on an audience – whether in the sense of the long-term political effect, of the emotional/rational effect of a single moment, or of the relationship between these two. The greater part of Bond's theorizing about his own and other people's dramaturgy is predicated on this single question: what will the theatre do to those who watch it? In a poem published in 1987 entitled (aptly enough) 'The Foyer of the Royal Court Theatre', he writes:

Drama is not an event in life such as buying a coat
It is an event about life – as the actor acts buying a coat the act asks:
    who are you who watch?
As you judge the play you judge yourself.

(P. 233)

He insists that the drama interrogates the audience as much as the audience interrogates the drama. Scene 6 of *Saved* is dramatically constructed so as to initiate this reciprocal interrogation, and what makes it so hard to sit through is the sense of powerlessness which it engenders, the growing knowledge that the process is murderous and that it cannot be stopped. Fred tries, briefly and feebly, to do so, and in doing so he attracts the audience's empathy. Soon, however, he gives up, and any hopes the audience might have invested in him are dashed. Eventually he reluctantly joins in – making the scene even more horrific, since he is probably the child's father, the one who should be protecting it. Worse, in a later scene, we discover that Len has watched the whole business.

LEN. I saw
FRED. What?
LEN. I come back when I couldn't find 'er.
FRED. Yer ain't grassed?
LEN. No.
FRED. O.
LEN. I was in the trees. I saw the pram.
FRED. Yeh.
LEN. I saw the lot.
FRED. Yeh.
LEN. I didn't know what t'do. Well, I should a stopped yer.

(P1 87)

Up to this point Len – like Scopey in *The Pope's Wedding* – has seemed to be the character to whom the audience can most easily relate, the focalizing character through whose eyes the world of the play is viewed. He is not completely different from the other characters in this bleak south London environment, but on the whole he is good-natured where others are surly, willing to help where others are out for themselves, generous where others are mean. He is the character with whom the audience is most clearly encouraged to identify. But now, as with Scopey, the audience finds that identification problematic, for Len (like them) watched the killing of the child and did nothing to prevent it. To the extent that the audience has allowed itself to share Len's point of view, then, it becomes implicated in his sin of omission. It may be a cliché to say that we are all in some way responsible for the atrocities which are committed in our society and sometimes in our name. But by using Fred and Len as onlookers to the violence whose inaction is clearly culpable, and by this means building a bridge between the horror of the on-stage action and the passivity of the viewing audience, Bond brings that commonplace to life: 'as you judge the play you judge yourself'. Ironically, it is from this moment on that Len begins to learn something about his own situation.

Scene 6, then, is shocking in itself. In another sense, though, equally shocking is the way it is contextualized within the play. It may be that what most disturbed the original critics and audiences was the fact that the rest of the play does not turn on this scene. The dramatic power of it is overwhelming: the scene's content ensures that. Yet in the narrative it is presented as merely one incident among many, and in much of the later part of the play the incident itself is rarely referred to directly, except by Len, whose anxious attempts to understand why it happened once more aligns him with the audience. Fred serves his sentence and is released, and things carry on much as before, with Pam still obsessed with Fred, Fred still uninterested in Pam, Len still trying to find a role in some sort of family with Pam. The narrative's attention is turned towards the complex and bitter pattern of emotional relationships within Pam's parents' house, where she and Len are still living, and where her parents, Harry and Mary, are playing out the endgame of a Strindbergian marriage. Len is drawn into this in an unexpected

15

way, which comprises Bond's oblique and darkly comic take on the Oedipus myth. Repeatedly rejected by Pam, Len ends up flirting with, and then having masturbatory fantasies about, Mary, her mother. The downtrodden Harry's knowledge of their putative relationship leads to a confrontation between him and Mary, in which Harry accuses her of 'goin' with 'er own daughter's left-overs'. They fight and a chair is broken: another moment of violence. The final scene of the play shows the family sitting down quietly and getting on with their everyday lives as Len (who had been about to leave the house, but eventually decided to stay) mends the broken chair. It is because of this simple gesture that Bond described the play at the time as being 'almost irresponsibly optimistic' (*P1* 309).

This provocative remark of Bond's is a good example of how his commentaries on his own plays frequently operate. What he says here works not so much as a final interpretation, cutting off further debate, but more as a stimulus to further argument. Typically, it produces indignant argument: how can a play which contains such horrors and so much bleakness possibly be called 'optimistic'? But this then opens up the debate, and in the course of that debate it may become clear that there *is* an optimism in *Saved*: not so much in the totality of its characters' lives – which are seen to be fatally impoverished – as in the suggestion that something might just be done about that impoverishment. Len's mending of the chair, clearly, operates as a kind of metaphor. It shifts the play's discourse onto a more symbolic plane than that which it seems at first to inhabit, representing some continuing attempt to make the human relationships of the play work, despite all the odds against it. But it is not only here, in the play's last moments, that the audience is asked to read the stage in symbolic–metaphoric terms. (If it were, it might seem a rather weak gesture in the face of what has gone before – almost an abdication of dramatic responsibility.) But the point is that this ambiguity of mode is typical of the play. Although the dominant mode of *Saved*, like that of *The Pope's Wedding*, appears to be naturalistic, there are actually other things going on on-stage as well. When the boys have killed the baby in the pram, they leave the stage emitting 'a curious buzzing' like a swarm of flies or bees. Bond would later call this kind of effect a 'Theatre Event' – something which goes

16

beyond the story which is being told and is not contained by it –
but in 1966 he had no such theory to describe it. Nonetheless,
even at its most basic level, it signals to an audience that
something beyond the obvious is happening on the stage. The
killing of the child in the pram (a child which, significantly,
never cries) is a piece of theatre designed to be understood
simultaneously as naturalistic and symbolic. It is simultaneously
an event in the 'lives' of these fictional characters, *and* a symbolic
image of a society which is already suffering from a kind of
spiritual death.

Brilliant though *Saved* is, it is not an entirely successful play in
Bond's own terms. This is not – as some might suggest – because
the low-key 'optimism' of the play's final moments is insufficient
to balance the trauma of the play's earlier violence. The smallness
of the gesture of mending the chair does not diminish its
theatrical power: indeed, the fact that it is such a small and
concentrated gesture is part of its intensity. The problem with
Saved is connected to a problem which Bond himself articulated
in connection with *The Pope's Wedding*:

> when I started to write I simply recorded, very much recorded, my
> experiences...[The earliest plays] were all, so far as I remem-
> ber...simply describing the world I'd grown up in or was living in,
> and I had this idea that if I described it clearly and accurately, then
> people would say 'Well, these things are terrible and we must do
> something about it'. Well, when I did produce my first play they
> didn't say that at all. They said 'How disgraceful, how dare you put
> these things on stage. How dare you show us these things?'[12]

In *Saved*, Bond was beginning to develop beyond simply
'showing these things', but had not yet discovered how to
stage a dramatic analysis of them. This was the search on which
he was now embarking.

A BROADER CANVAS: *EARLY MORNING* AND *NARROW ROAD*

The Pope's Wedding and *Saved*, both contain the beginnings of
Bond's search for a more complex dramatic language than that
which naturalism could offer. After *Saved* this search led him
away both from contemporary settings, and even further from

the conventions of domestic naturalism with which he had begun. It may be that the critical reaction to *Saved* prompted this move away from the social realism of those early plays. It does seem to have instilled in him a firm conviction that if he wanted his plays to have any effect on the world he was living in, it was not going to be enough simply to describe that world.

> I'd rather sort of assumed that there were enough people in society –
> if you could actually tell them what's going on [who] would do
> something about it, [but] no, you got into this whole series of excuses
> like 'It's their fault' or 'They were born like that' or 'There is
> nothing we can do about it but punish them for being like that' and
> things like that. So then it became necessary for me to understand
> the situation more and to see why things went wrong...And my
> plays since then have been an exploration of the problems of being a
> human being in the twentieth century and to try to find out why
> things go wrong and how we could correct them.[13]

This exploration started in earnest in *Early Morning* (1968), an extraordinary, open-textured play set in a surreal landscape which is something like Victorian England. In it George and Arthur (two mythically English names) are Siamese twins and also the heirs to the throne of Queen Victoria, who become embroiled in civil wars engineered by Prince Albert and Gladstone. Victoria herself, a clownish tyrant who carries on a clandestine love affair with a cross-dressed Florence Nightingale, is a theatrical second cousin to Jarry's Père Ubu, and the play's world is made up of a disturbing collage of historical reference, contemporary society, and dreamlike fantasy.

The theme of linked opposites is a central concept in the play, not only in the striking central image of the Siamese twins, but also because the action elaborates on the notion of 'two worlds', taking place first of all on earth and then in heaven, where all the characters meet once more after they die. The horror, however, continues there, for the vision of heaven which this play presents is a grotesque one, in which earthly violence is translated into celestial cannibalism. For Arthur, who becomes the play's central character, earth and heaven are both nightmares from which he is trying to wake up. Eventually he succeeds: the final image shows him, like a Christ figure, ascending not into heaven, but out of it and beyond it.

Like Len and Scopey, Arthur is another Bondian hero searching for some understanding: more specifically, he is searching for his own humanity in an inhuman world. In this surreal theatre, however, the effects are exaggerated. In *Saved* a child was killed; in *Early Morning* people eat each other *en masse*. Scopey killed an old man, Arthur goes mad and engineers mass slaughter. Yet, paradoxically, because of the play's generally grotesque mode, audiences often find Arthur easier to accept as a moral centre than Bond's earlier heroes. The experiments with form which Bond undertook in *Early Morning* also gave him an opportunity to create characters who could directly articulate a more sophisticated vision of the world than those in his earlier plays, and Arthur, in his journey through madness and sanity, touches on what was to become one of the central ideas of Bond's plays – the interrelatedness of good and evil:

> Why do men hate life? Is it the light? Is it more comfortable to be mud and ashes?...Not many people rise to the height of Hitler. Most of them only nurse little hates. They kill under licence. Doctor, Hitler had vision. He knew we hated ourselves, and each other, so out of charity he let us kill and be killed...Heil Hitler! Heil Einstein! Hitler gets a bad name, and Einstein's good. But it doesn't matter, the good still kill. And the civilized kill more than the savage.

> (P1 186)

Early Morning is one of Bond's most disturbing plays, but it is also one of his funniest. Its proposed first production was banned in its entirety by the Lord Chamberlain, the script being returned with the comment that 'His Lordship would not allow it'. The ensuing row threw the Royal Court into crisis, and the play did not receive a full public performance until 1969. By now Bond's fame as a playwright was resting largely on the basis of plays which had been banned.

His admirers, however, included those within the so-called establishment. *Narrow Road to the Deep North*, his next play, was first performed at the Belgrade Theatre Coventry, having been commissioned by Canon Steven Verney of Coventry Cathedral for performance as part of the 1968 People and Cities Conference. It is difficult to know quite what the conference expected: Bond's notoriety as the author of *Saved* might well have led them to imagine that he would offer them another play set in the bleakness of contemporary south London.

19

Instead, they got a story which is set in feudal Japan and which starts out as a parable about personal salvation and social obligation, telling how a Buddhist poet searching for enlightenment fails to rescue an abandoned baby (who may be another version of the child from *Saved*). The theme of cities is subsumed into a larger meditation on the workings of power and morality, focused on the character of Shogo, a tyrannical city governor who the audience is led to believe – although it is never definitively stated – is the abandoned baby grown to manhood. The mood of the play, however, shifts quickly from parable to parody with the entrance of Georgina and the Commodore, caricatured nineteenth-century British imperialists set on conquering the city, who generate a series of scenes which are very reminiscent in tone of *Early Morning*.

Bond was never completely happy with *Narrow Road*, which apparently took him only three days to write. It did, however, bring him much wider acceptance as a writer. Within two years of its première, it had received over twenty other productions in Britain, continental Europe (both Eastern and Western), North America and New Zealand. It was during this period, too, that *Saved* began to be performed more widely. In 1969, following the Theatres Act which abolished theatre censorship in the UK, the Royal Court staged a season of Bond's plays, and his position as a major dramatist was established.

Bond, then, had moved well away from whatever roots he might have had in domestic naturalism, and was now beginning to develop a strategy of staging his vision of the present through the medium of historical and cultural periods deliberately distant from his own. The fictional worlds he created were unstable ones, packed with anachronisms: the nineteenth-century world of *Early Morning* includes cinemas, radio telephones and references to Hitler and Einstein. Basho's seventeenth-century Japanese monks and poets come into conflict with Victorian imperialists and civil servants, and the play eventually turns out to be set in an indeterminate era which includes both the seventeenth and the nineteenth centuries. This instability has the effect of keeping the audience off-balance. Like Brecht's 'Alienation-effect', it forces an audience continually to review the perspective from which they are understanding events. Bond, of course, has frequently been compared to Brecht, and there are certainly various theatrical links between these two socialist playwrights, not least of which is the fact that William Gaskill, Bond's earliest regular director and champion at the Royal Court, was also known in the early sixties as the 'leading British director of Brecht'.[14] In 1970, Bond undertook a translation and adaptation of Brecht's *The Round-heads and The Peakheads*. This has never had a full professional production, although it was given a rehearsed reading in 1976. It was, however, a good way for Bond to get to know more about Brecht's dramatic techniques.

At this time, for Bond – as for many left-wing British playwrights – the growing theatrical vogue of Brechtian and pseudo-Brechtian ideas was as much a problem as it was an inspiration. Like many of his generation, Bond had seen the first London productions of Brecht's 'epic' plays by the Berliner Ensemble, and had found them exhilarating. But in the UK there was much misinformation about Brecht's ideas, the majority of which remained untranslated or available only in unreliable translations. English 'Brechtianism' frequently amounted to a generally prescriptive misapprehension that left-wing theatre should deal only in historical abstractions, not in human subjectivity, and that its form should be clinical, 'objective' in the sense of 'impersonal', and devoid of emotion. (This in turn derived from prevalent assumptions about the historical determinism of Marxist thought in general.) As a result, Bond's early instincts were to be suspicious of the 'Brechtian' label. Probably, too, a rejection of such influence was necessary for him personally, in order to allow him room to grow as an artist. In any case, what is most significant is the extent to which Bond made what he learned from Brecht his own.

A paradigm for this might be the image of the abandoned or threatened child. Brecht uses this famously in *The Caucasian Chalk Circle* – one of the plays which the Berliner brought to London in 1956, and the play with which, in his 1962 production for the RSC, Gaskill made his name as the leading British Brechtian. In *Chalk Circle*, Grusha, the servant girl escaping from the war-torn city, is left – literally – holding the baby, as the fleeing princes abandon their infant son to her care. Although it endangers her own safety and happiness, Grusha takes the child with her and devotes herself to caring for it. The Singer,

21

narrating the story, comments 'Terrible is the temptation to do good!' This image of the abandoned or threatened child becomes a key one in Bond's plays. From *Narrow Road* onwards, he comes back to it again and again in plays such as *The Bundle, Jackets, Great Peace, Tuesday* and *At the Inland Sea* – sometimes dealing with it centrally and directly, and sometimes more obliquely. (If one includes, too, Bond's own early and very different use of the image in *Saved*, as well as some of the grown-up children in Bond's later plays, such as the Young Woman in *Bingo*, Ismene in *The Woman*, or The Girl in *Coffee*, it becomes clear just how central this image of the threatened child has been to Bond's larger narrative.)

Moreover Brecht's problem of the 'terrible...temptation to do good' (which is articulated in *The Caucasian Chalk Circle* and *The Good Person of Szechwan*) also becomes a repeated motif in Bond's plays. The conclusions to which Bond comes are not, however, always the same as Brecht's. Grusha picks up the child and thereby affirms her humanity, but in Bond's work it may be the refusal to act like Grusha which is the index of a character's humanity. In the same way, Bond's wider dramaturgical theory and practice owe something to a relationship to Brechtian theatre which amounts not so much to 'influence' as to a dialectic. Where Brecht developed theories of performance based on his 'alienation effects', Bond replied with his concept of the 'aggro-effect' designed to commit an audience emotionally and thus to jolt it into questioning the realities which it might normally accept uncritically. Bond even annexes the famous Brechtian term 'epic theatre', redefining it for his own purposes:

> This name is often misunderstood, partly because the form isn't yet fully developed. An epic play tells a story and says why it happened. This gives it a beginning, a middle and an end joined together in a truthful way...Epic plays don't need to cover centuries or have a cast of armies. The essence of epic theatre is the way it selects, connects and judges. (*P4* 108)

Selecting, connecting and judging were to become key concepts in Bond's own dramaturgy.

SHAKESPEAREAN VARIATIONS: *LEAR* AND *THE SEA*

A central theme of Bond's work has always been the relationship between the past and the present. William Gaskill recalls some of the early, unpublished and unperformed work which the young Bond submitted to the Royal Court Theatre: Bond 'had been invited to join the [Royal Court Theatre Writer's] Group because of a play he had submitted called *Klaxon in Atreus' Palace* which I couldn't understand at all but Keith [Johnstone] had liked. With hindsight I suppose its title implied "I'm going to show these ancient Greeks what a working class writer can do"'.[15] If Gaskill is right about the meaning of the title, then even in the earliest phases of his career Bond's attitude to the classics of Western theatrical tradition was essentially combative, challenging the cultural hegemony on its own ground. In his next major work Bond deliberately took on one of the sacred cows of the British cultural establishment: he rewrote a Shakespeare play. More, he rewrote *King Lear*.

Bond's *Lear* (1971), a play once more epic in both scope and style, was born out of a passionate 'argument' with Shakespeare's play, a sense that *King Lear* was too big, too important, to be left alone, and that the messages which it offered to contemporary culture needed to be challenged. 'Lear was standing in my path,' he explained, 'and I had to get him out of the way. I couldn't get beyond him to do other things that I also wanted, so I had to come to terms with him'.[16] The stage world of *Lear* is another of Bond's unstable universes, clearly both related to our own and also a composite of several others. The power which Lear wields at the beginning of the play is effectively feudal, while the technology of violence in the play is very up to date: soldiers carry guns, and the prison doctor works in a modern laboratory. (This unstable mixture of periods is also true, of course, of Shakespeare's play.) Bond retains the basic narrative structure of *King Lear*: an authoritarian ruler loses power, then comes into bloody conflict with his daughters, unleashing a tide of civil and personal violence. However, most of the features of Shakespeare's play, are radically altered, and Bond makes the story very much his own. There is, for example, no sub-plot to counterbalance the horrors through which Lear passes, no heroic Edgar to lurk in disguise on the heath and to

23

turn up at the last minute to vanquish evildoers in mortal combat, nor any loving followers or redemptive daughter to battle for his life; Bond's Cordelia is a more ruthless force altogether. Goneril and Regan become Bodice and Fontanelle: considering their upbringing by Lear, it is not surprising that they have become every bit as evil and vicious as Shakespeare's originals, but they also bring with them some of the comic energy of Victoria and Georgina from *Early Morning* and *Narrow Road*. The comedy of the play revolves around its vicious characters: Bond's Lear has no witty and wise fool to accompany him on his journey through madness, but only a sad, lost ghost who follows him around.

Shakespeare's *King Lear* is regularly quoted in arguments about the representation of violence on the stage. While death and maiming are the stock-in-trade of Elizabethan and Jacobean tragedy, there is something particularly graphic about the on-stage blinding of Gloucester; the scene in which an old man is tied to a chair as his eyes are put out by a sadistic nobleman while his ghoulish wife looks on and encourages him is (rightly) pointed out as one of the most brutal in the classical repertoire. It is hard, too, to talk about Bond's *Lear* without reverting to questions about the violence of the play. Bond himself began his 'Preface to *Lear*' with the acknowledgement that

> I write about violence as naturally as Jane Austen did about manners. Violence shapes and obsesses our society and if we do not stop being violent we have no future ... It would be immoral not to write about violence. (P2 3)

It is a belief which he continues to hold.

As the play opens Bond's Lear, far from planning to give away his kingdom in order to crawl unburdened towards death, is obsessed with holding his country together, with protecting it from invasion by his enemies. But his daughters, Fontanelle and Bodice, marry those very enemies, and the kingdom is cast into civil war. Lear's adviser, Warrington, is captured by Fontanelle and Bodice, and mutilated, while Lear becomes a fugitive, finding temporary refuge in the house of a gravedigger's son and his wife. But Bodice and Fontanelle's soldiers arrive, killing the Gravedigger's Boy and raping his wife – whose name, we now learn, is Cordelia. They capture Lear and take him back to stand trial. However, during the time of his imprisonment a further civil war erupts. A guerrilla army, led by Cordelia eventually overcomes the forces of Bodice and Fontanelle. This, however, does not result in Lear's rescue. Bodice and Fontanelle are killed, but this Cordelia has no love for Lear. On her orders he is blinded and (like Shakespeare's Gloucester) put out to stumble around the countryside. Accompanied by the ghost of the Gravedigger's Boy, he finds his way back to their old house, and lives there with a new community which is growing up there. Once more he seems to have found some kind of refuge here; he achieves fame and a following as the teller of politically loaded parables. But when Cordelia visits him to try and prevent him from telling his subversive stories, his time of peace ends. The ghost of the boy 'dies' (for the second time) and Lear makes his final gesture: he journeys back to the wall which he built around his kingdom, and is shot trying to dismantle it.

Bond has, on several occasions, stated why he felt the need to engage – and quarrel – with Shakespeare's play:

> The social moral of Shakespeare's *Lear* is this: endure till in time the world will be made right. That's a dangerous moral for us. We have less time than Shakespeare.[17]

> Shakespeare says that Lear's suffering and partial, ineffective illumination represent the fallible condition of all human goodness. The problem is seen to be political but the solution given isn't – it recommends calmness and acceptance. (*P4* 126)

> As Shakespeare himself knew, the peace, the reconciliation that he created on the stage would not last an hour on the street. (*P2* p. x)

And in Bond's *Lear*, peace and reconciliation are continually shown to be illusory. If Shakespeare's play contains images of extreme violence, the violence in Bond's version is almost overwhelming. The action of the play is structured around a sequence of violent stage images: a workman is killed by accident, another executed; troops march to war; the captured Warrington is mutilated by Bodice and Fontanelle; now insane, Warrington attacks and wounds Lear; soldiers rape Cordelia, capture Lear, and kill Warrington and the Gravedigger's Boy; the Carpenter in turn kills four of the soldiers; a captured soldier is executed by Cordelia's men while another soldier dies of his wounds; Fontanelle is shot, and her body autopsied; Bodice is bayoneted to death by soldiers; Lear's eyes are put out; the ghost of the boy dies, gored by pigs; Lear is shot and killed.

The parade of killing and mutilation seems, like the horrors in *Early Morning*, to be incessant and inescapable. Yet to say this is to do an injustice to the play's dramatic texture, for the variety of tone within this parade is remarkable. Take, for example, the mutilation of Warrington – a horrendous scene, made all the more ghoulish by the pantomime-dame performances of Bodice and Fontanelle as they encourage, and participate in, Warrington's punishment. Fontanelle jumps up and down, shouting gleefully: 'Throw him up and drop him. I want to hear him drop...Kill his hands, kill his feet...'I've always wanted to sit on a man's lungs' (P2 28). The little-girl excitement of her language contrasts comically and disturbingly with the horrors being enacted on the courtier. Meanwhile, Bodice sits calmly by and knits, eventually joining in to enact a charade whereby the soldier who is torturing Warrington is made to plead for his life so that she can refuse ('That always gives me my deepest satisfaction' P2 29). Then, deciding that Warrington needs to be 'shut up inside himself', she pokes her knitting needles into his ears, saying 'I'll just jog these in and out a little. Doodee, doodee, doodee, doo' (P2 29). Again, it is the counterpoint between the cosy and the domestic and the horrors of the torture which is both very funny and utterly unnerving. In *Lear* the ways in which the moments of violence are staged are themselves analyses of violence.

This effect is later picked up and used again in the scene in which Lear himself is blinded – by the Fourth Prisoner, acting as the prison doctor. The scene enacts a parody of Lear's former royalty: his robes are translated into a straitjacket, and a square frame which fits over his head and eyes is referred to as his crown. The relationship between violence and technology is a recurring theme in Bond's writings, and the eye-extracting machine is a powerful symbol of the dehumanizing uses of technology. But the issue is not simply that technology is 'bad'. More to the point is the question which was articulated in Arthur's Hitler/Einstein speech in *Early Morning*. It is not technology itself but the uses to which it can be put which are so horrific. This is underlined by the language which the prisoner-turned-doctor speaks: he describes his own brutality calmly and dispassionately, in a pseudo-scientific language which has completely lost contact with any human reality: 'With this device you can extract the eye undamaged and then it can be put to good use. It's based on a scouting gadget I had as a boy...Note how the eye passes into the lower chamber and is received into a soothing solution of formaldehyde crystals' (*P2* 77). The joke about scouting gadgets is an easy one at the expense of that paramilitary youth organization. The description of the solution of formaldehyde (for the disembodied eye) as 'soothing', however, is a more deep-rooted jibe at the disjunction between language and actuality which is typical of science when it is in the service of military power. It is this same impulse which leads, in the language of contemporary conflict, to phrases such as 'friendly fire' and 'decommissioning personnel'.

There is, however, another moment earlier in the same scene, where the violence creates an utterly different effect. After Fontanelle has been brutally executed, Lear peers at the corpse of his treacherous daughter as it is cut open for autopsy. An audience might be expected to find such a moment repulsive – but that reaction is turned against itself, and the scene becomes strangely moving, as Lear marvels at the extraordinary beauty of the body:

> She sleeps inside like a lion and a lamb and a child. The things are so beautiful. I am astonished. I have never seen anything so beautiful. If I had known she was so beautiful...Her body was made by the hand of a child, so sure and nothing unclean...If I had known this beauty and patience and care, how I would have loved her.   (*P2* 73)

Here both the language and the stage picture create a different kind of dramatic juxtaposition – or rather a series of dramatic juxtapositions – as the father looks at the dead daughter: death and life, beauty and ugliness, violence and stillness, childhood and adulthood, the 'innocence' of the dead woman as against her murderousness when she was alive. Bond here takes his cue directly from one of Shakespeare's lines. When the original Lear is losing his sanity, the Shakespearean king proclaims, 'Let them anatomize Regan; see what breeds about her heart. Is there any cause in Nature that makes these hard-hearts?' (*King Lear*, III. 6). Bond takes this image and, first of all, expands it – in earlier scenes his Lear had been obsessively searching for the 'beast' which dwells within humans and makes them cruel and vicious. But as Lear continues this search, Bond also literalizes Shakespeare's image: the king's daughter is indeed anatomized, and when Lear peers into her and sees no beast but simply the marvel of the human body, an extraordinary and dramatic *coup de théâtre* is performed. The ugliness of the dissected body gives way to a sense of wonder; it is a rare moment of tenderness in the play. The irony of it is that Lear is only able to respond to Fontanelle's beauty (and perhaps Fontanelle is only able to *be* beautiful) in death.

A powerful visual symbol in *Lear* is the high wall which Lear's soldiers are building at the beginning of the play in order to keep his enemies out, and with which Lear is totally preoccupied. A soldier whose clumsiness briefly interrupts work on the wall is summarily executed and Lear explains

> I started this wall when I was young. I stopped my enemies in the field but there were always more of them. How could we ever be free? So I built this wall to keep our enemies out. My people will live behind this wall when I'm dead...My wall will make you free. (P2 17–18)

The wall, clearly, represents not so much a protection from the enemies beyond as the way in which Lear has imprisoned both himself and his people. By the end of the play, Lear has been imprisoned, blinded, and exiled; his country has been torn apart by civil wars, resulting eventually in the rise to power of a Cordelia who is not, in this version of the story, Lear's daughter at all, but a charismatic figure who is a cross between Che Guevara and Stalin – a ruthless revolutionary leader who, in the name of freedom, looks set to repeat the oppressions of Lear's own reign.

Significantly the audience does not actually see Lear's wall until the final scene of the play; up to this point its presence and importance has been established only by verbal reference. When it *is* made visible, it is so that something can, finally, be done about it. Lear's last action is one of both destruction and self-destruction: he dies mounting a lone assault on the wall which he himself started to build. The hopelessness of the action is clear, yet the gesture is an optimistic one. His attack on the wall shows him taking responsibility for the culture of death which

he created and which Cordelia can only perpetuate. In contrast
to the private tragic illumination of Shakespeare's Lear, Bond's
Lear dies performing a gesture which is simultaneously personal
and political.

Lear remains one of Bond's most important and influential
works, and since 'all previous plays prepare you to write the
next play' (*T.* 55) it became also an essential point of departure
for several plays which he wrote over the next few years. In 1973
two new Bond plays were produced: *The Sea* at the Royal Court
in May, and *Bingo* at the Northcott Theatre, Exeter, in November.
Both of these, in different ways, grew out of *Lear*, and both used
more conventional structures and period settings, without the
insistence on anachronism and dislocation of his earlier 'history'
plays. The action of *The Sea* takes place in the shadow of a fatal
boating accident and the central characters are Rose, the drowned
man's fiancée, and Willy, his best friend. Despite this sombre
background *The Sea* is essentially a class comedy. The events
portrayed include tragic matter, but Bond is insistent that the
play *is* a comedy and that it 'should be played lightly'.[18] It is set
in 1907 in a small English seaside town, and peopled by various
eccentrics. There is the imperious Mrs Rafi, with her tendency to
utter Wildean epigrams; the reclusive Evens; and the mad
draper Hatch, who has convinced the local coastguards that they
are in the process of being invaded by Martians. As the unusual
spelling of both their names might suggest, Evens is a distant
descendant of Alen from *The Pope's Wedding*, and Willy visits him
repeatedly in the way that Scopey visited Alen. The difference in
this play, however, is that Evens, unlike Alen, *does* have some
special knowledge, a vision of the universe more profound than
that of the other characters. His final speech to Willy imparts
some of this, but he also adds 'Don't trust the wise fool too
much. What he knows matters and you die without it. But he
never knows enough...' (*P2* 168–9).

In a review of the first production, the critic Martin Esslin
made suggestive connections between *The Sea* and *Lear*.

> After Bond's *Lear*... one is tempted to think that *The Sea* might be
> something like his *Tempest*... But then one could also argue that *The
> Sea* resumes the great solemn and violent theme of *Lear* and varies it
> in the mode of a scherzo. Hatch madly tramping along the shore,
> driven insane by the world' s cruelty, is a harmless comic version of

mad Lear, the stately Mrs. Rafi, statuesque queen-bee of her little seaside town and her rival and sidekick Mrs. Tilehouse, would then appear as attenuated versions of the wicked sisters, Bodice and Fontanelle, while the pure and perceptive Rose Jones, who loses her fiancé in the storm and finally comes to love his friend who was saved, has features of Bond's Cordelia... In both plays madness and dehumanization of man are the main themes – on a heroic and barbaric scale in *Lear*, in the small domestic framework of the English class system in *The Sea*.[19]

The details of Esslin's interpretation may be debatable (Hatch is much more than a 'harmless comic version' of anything, while the implied reading of Bond's Cordelia as 'pure and perceptive' is extraordinary). Nonetheless, Esslin rightly points to some of the thematic continuities between these two apparently very different plays. *The Sea* deals with many of the issues which Bond had been looking at in *Lear*. If the tone is lighter, the play still conjures up a claustrophobic world in which people destroy themselves and each other. The ending optimistically allows Rose and Willy to escape from the town, as Evens tells Willy, 'You won't find any more answers here. Go away and find them...I've told you these things so that you won't despair. But you must still change the world' (*P2* 169). But the world which Willy is being charged with the duty of changing will erupt in a few years' time in the First World War. His unfinished reply turns out to be the last line of the play: 'I came to say goodbye, and I'm glad you –' (*P2* 169). The truncated nature of the line creates a moment of silence, an unresolved cadence at the end of the play:

> The play ends in the way that it does – moving from the uproar of the storm to the still silence...because it is a TE handing the play to the audience. The stillness should be held just long enough for the audience to stop staring at 'them' and realize that they [i.e. the audience] are part of the image and so the play and its celebration of life is made theirs.[20]

BOND AND THE ROYAL COURT THEATRE

Throughout this period, Bond was one of the playwrights associated in the mind of the theatregoing public with the Royal Court Theatre, with which he enjoyed a fruitful association. The formation of the Writers' Group had brought into the Court a new and politically aware group of people. Many of the Court's 'old guard' were still in residence during the sixties, but the Writers' Group quite correctly thought of itself as being at the centre of the Court's work. It was at least partly because of the work done through this group that the Court became a place in which productive relationships between individual writers and resident Court directors were able to evolve. From December 1962 until November 1975, only two of Bond's major plays – *Narrow Road to the Deep North* (Coventry) and *Bingo* (Exeter) – did not open at the Royal Court; and *Narrow Road* transferred there eight months after its Coventry opening. Nearly all these Royal Court productions were directed by William Gaskill, whose comment on their working relationship is illuminating:

> I've always sought those writers whose work I could identify with and I was lucky to find, even for a brief period, a writer like Edward Bond of whom that was true. Even with Bond I only felt that absolute certainty with *Saved* and started to diverge from him in his later plays. Perhaps this was also connected with Edward's increasing need to have a more direct control over the production. When I turned down *The Fool* in 1975 it was directed by Peter Gill, himself a writer, who has his own personal use of theatre imagery and was bound to conflict with Bond. Ever since, with the exception of *Bingo* and *The Bundle*, Bond has directed his own plays.[21]

Significantly, one of the points of divergence between Bond and Gaskill at the Royal Court involved Bond's increasingly overt dramatization of a socialist politics.

The relationship between Bond and the English Stage Company at the Royal Court was not always a comfortable nor a trouble-free one. Quite apart from his deteriorating working relationship with Gaskill, Bond had always had his detractors as well as his supporters in the building. Even George Devine, the Court's founder and inspiration, had never really understood Bond's plays, while others there were positively antagonistic. At the time of *Early Morning*, when the Lord Chamberlain was refusing to allow the play a licence, and Gaskill was determined to continue into production anyway, Bond's and Gaskill's antagonists resided in the Court itself as much as anywhere, and demands were made (unsuccessfully) for the suspension of Gaskill as artistic director because of his unwavering support for the play.

Nonetheless, the Royal Court provided Bond with a 'home' for much of his early play-writing career. It offered him security and a (mainly) supportive environment which enabled him to experiment and to grow as a writer. Bond paid tribute to the Court in a 1972 interview, saying 'I couldn't have worked in any other theatre. To begin with there's no other English theatre that would have produced my plays'.[22] But even as Bond acknowledged the importance of the relationship, it was nearing its end, and after Peter Gill's 1975 production of *The Fool*, Bond and the Court parted company almost completely as far as his new writing was concerned. Bond has returned there only intermittently: in 1979 he directed a youth theatre production of *The Worlds* and in 1981, a full production of *Restoration*; at the time of writing, in 1997, a Welsh community theatre's production of *Coffee* is being staged there. But the close relationship which existed between the writer and the institution did not last beyond the mid-seventies. A new generation of radical writers was to flourish there in the next few years as Max Stafford-Clark took over the artistic directorship, but for Bond the Royal Court came to represent something essentially backward-looking.

2

Questions and Answers

Nowadays art is often dismissed as irrelevant to the solution of social problems. It will be clear that I don't believe this. If creative imagination exists in all people, it must have a use. (P3 77)

TWO POETS: *BINGO* AND *THE FOOL*

By the time he had written *The Sea*, Bond found that he had come to a kind of *impasse*: that first series of plays was not, after all, to comprise his life's work. Rather it had unearthed the issues which he needed to explore further. And so

> I decided that I would write a series of plays which dealt specifically with this problem of culture, with the problem of the burden of the past which makes a change so difficult: these plays were *Bingo*, *The Fool* and *The Woman*.[1]

With another unmistakable reference to Shakespeare, Bond himself has described these as his 'problem plays'. Each of the three plays looks at society at a crucial moment of its development. The first of them, *Bingo* (1973), continues Bond's preoccupation with Shakespeare as a cultural force. Here Bond imagines Shakespeare in the last months of his life, in his garden at New Place, and draws on documentary evidence of Shakespeare's involvement in the enclosures of the common land around Stratford which ruined many smallholders. The focus of the play is the split which Bond postulates must have existed between the moral vision of Shakespeare's artistic creation and the compromises which he made in real life.

Bingo asks once more some of the questions about the moral authority of the poet which had first been raised with the character of Basho in *Narrow Road* – although in fact Bond paints a far more sympathetic picture of Shakespeare than he had done of Basho. In *Bingo*, Shakespeare takes on the function of the characteristic Bond hero, watching and trying to understand a world distorted by cruelty. One of the significant things about Bond's Shakespeare is how little he speaks. The language which had made him famous is now deserting him. When Ben Jonson brings news of the burning of the Globe theatre, he tries to find out what Shakespeare is now writing, but is unable or unwilling to accept Shakespeare's simple answer: 'Nothing...Nothing to say' (*P3* 42). And this 'nothing to say' is part of the problem. It is in his silences, in his inability or unwillingness to speak out against the injustices which play themselves out around him, that Shakespeare's 'crime' lies. Bond locates the play as firmly as he can in the known facts of early seventeenth-century Warwickshire, although much of the detail is inevitably conjectural. The landowner, Combe, schemes to get richer by enclosing the fields around Stratford. A revolutionary Puritan movement, a little like the historical Diggers, arises briefly in reaction against the enclosures. Agricultural labourers carry out small acts of sabotage. Innocent victims suffer in the process: a vagrant girl is abused, whipped, and hanged.

The early seventeenth century was a period of nascent capitalism in England; mercantile expansionism was leading to a new economic and monetary order – this was a constant theme of the playwrights and satirists of the time, Shakespeare included. The writers complained that the world was changing, that old feudal loyalties, rights and duties, and old traditions, were disappearing, being swallowed up by the new acquisitive culture with its emphasis on the importance of money. Bond is doing nothing out of the ordinary in portraying the world of Shakespeare in this light. What made audiences uncomfortable about the play, though, was that in *Bingo* Bond portrayed Shakespeare as being implicated in that social order and its resultant barbarisms, not transcending it because of his special knowledge or art. In this, incidentally, Bond pre-empts much academic criticism of Shakespeare, especially that of the new historicist and cultural materialist schools, which began in the 1980s to examine critically the political contexts of Shakespeare's writing. In *Bingo*, the man whose plays analysed and exposed the cruelties of the world finds himself a part of those

34

same oppressive processes. And so, for all his insight, for all his good intentions and his desire to do no harm, Shakespeare perceives that he is as implicated in the everyday cruelties of his society as anyone. He tries to show compassion to the vagrant girl, but she ends up on the gibbet anyway.

Bingo is subtitled *Scenes of Money and Death*, and Bond explains this subtitle as follows:

> I want to get away from the well-made play, and to do that I called *Bingo* 'scenes of something'. These scenes of something don't just tell a story, they also, I hope, make a statement to those watching, a statement the audience is invited to finish.[2]

The dramaturgical principle is clear: the aim is to engage the audience as meaning-makers, and the strategy is to construct a play in terms of a series of discrete but thematically linked scenes, to which meaning is given by their juxtaposition and ordering.

This principle is developed further in his next play, which is also about a poet in a rural setting. The very title of *The Fool* (1975) suggests a continuation of Bond's Shakespearean theme, but the fool in question is not Lear's jester, but the nineteenth-century 'peasant-poet' John Clare. The play is subtitled *Scenes of Bread and Love*, but whereas in *Bingo* the scenes from Shakespeare's life related to a period of twelve months or so leading up to Shakespeare's death, in *The Fool* Bond presents eight scenes which cover Clare's life, from his youth as an agricultural labourer, to his brief period of literary fame, to his death in a madhouse at the age of 70. The resultant time lapses, and the amount of information which the audience has to infer about Clare's life and career, are enormous. This technique subverts any expectations which an audience might have of being presented with a 'biographical' account or a historical reconstruction of Clare's life. It is particularly important for Bond to do this, since there are inevitable comparisons which could be drawn between John Clare and Bond himself: both came from working-class backgrounds, both received comparatively little formal education, and both had a radical perspective on their society which the establishment found troubling and attempted to censor. But any over-simple identification between Clare and Bond misses the point: if *The Fool* is partly about the role of the artist in society, it looks at that artist more as victim than as hero.

In fact, *The Fool* has as much to say about the wider effects of social changes during Britain's early industrial expansion as it does about the life of the poet. In the early scenes, in fact, Clare is almost anonymous. He emerges only slowly from the group of alienated and dispossessed agricultural workers on whose social existence the play initially concentrates. As he did in *Bingo*, Bond is dealing with a period of rural history which is marked by enclosures of common ground, and resulting in great hardship for the rural poor. But while Bond's Shakespeare was uncomfortably allied with the landowning gentry, his Clare is (again somewhat uncomfortably) allied with the agricultural workers who riot in protest at the enclosures, and who are eventually imprisoned and transported or – like Clare's close friend and brother-in-law Darkie – hanged as a result. Darkie is a complex figure. In Bond's plays there are frequently pairs of characters who function as aspects of each other (we have already seen Lear and his Ghost, Arthur and George) and Darkie is to some extent an aspect, or another version, of Clare himself – another casualty of an oppressive social system, who turns to violence rather than poetry and is destroyed because of it. Darkie also contains aspects of characters in other plays: for example, his rural activism connects him with the levelling activities of the puritan Son in *Bingo*, while he will reappear in another form as the Dark Man in *The Woman*.

Clare himself avoids the fate of his friends: while they are struggling with the political changes which have overtaken their world, he is obsessed by the elusive figure of Mary, a girl whom he idealizes and idolizes, and for whose memory he later neglects his wife, Patty. Clare's romantic and sexual obsession with Mary is symptomatic of his own increasing alienation from his social and material environment. Darkie ends up as a martyr, but Clare's fate is more complex and more contradictory. His writings, fuelled by the same understanding of the realities of rural England which led Darkie to the gallows, make him famous and he is briefly lionized by the London literary set. But his new status as the 'peasant-poet' also brings about contradictions which he is unable to resolve. Charles Lamb says, 'Clare tells the truth...[and] truth isn't governed by the laws of supply and demand...Truth shelters in the gutter. Only the man who stoops finds it' (P3 121). Inevitably, though, this truth-telling also leads to his patrons' and publishers' attempts to censor his work. As one of his financial backers, Admiral Lord Radstock, explains to Clare,

> I have one reservation. Not serious. The fault of a narrow horizon. Those remarks in – poem named after your village – which criticizes the landowning classes – smack of radicalism...I shan't lecture you. Political science isn't parish pump philosophy. But answer this. Who controls the brute in man? Polite society. Well, your verse undermines its authority. There'd be chaos. The poor would be the first to suffer. I understand some hangings have already been necessary in your part of the world. Makes my point for me. (P3 124–5)

Ironically, it is the authoritarian Radstock who articulates the connection between Clare's poetry and the enclosure riots and their bloody consequences. But Clare is unable to censor himself in the way Radstock requires. Like the wise Shakespearean fool, he must speak an unpalatable truth – and also like Shakespeare's fools, his licence is limited: he is soon dropped by fashionable London, and sinks back into his former obscurity. But he has been torn from his roots and is no longer able to function as a labourer. Once more a central character in a Bond play is caught between two worlds, and Clare is lost because of it. Lacking the self-awareness or the historical or political consciousness which would enable him to make sense of the contradictions both in his own life and in the society around him, he eventually goes mad. The play charts his progression from one sort of fool to another.

Radstock's speech above comes in one of the play's central scenes, whose structure suggests the economy and intensity of Bond's use of the stage in The Fool. It is set in Hyde Park (which another of his patrons, the gushing Mrs Emmerson, is convinced 'reminds Clare of his native country', P3 120). Downstage, Radstock and Mrs Emmerson tell Clare about his own poetry, while the drunken Charles Lamb makes incisive comments about the nature of truth, and his half-mad sister Mary talks obsessively about shopping for food which no longer satisfies her and which will rot uneaten on their floor. It is already a powerful picture of the complex world of artistic supply and demand which Clare has been drawn into – but it is juxtaposed with an even more telling image: upstage, a prize-fight is taking place. As Clare's circle quote and discuss literature, the fighters beat each other nearly senseless: but the point is not so much the difference between these two parts of the scene as the similarities between them. The prize-fight is a clear, brutal and stark image of the exploitative economic relationships of Clare's society, and the downstage action of cultured literary discussion is effectively shown to be a more sophisticated symptom of the same underlying structure. The prize-fight metaphor (which in fact derives from the historical Clare's own writings) is referred to and developed as the play progresses. Clare comes to recognize that he is as much the 'property' of his patrons as the pugilists, and that his pain, too, is paid for by them. In a later surreal scene, which takes place largely in Clare's own imagination, Clare tries to pick a fight with a shadowy figure of a boxer who turns out to be the hanged Darkie. The image makes a powerful connection between the two men, both as fighters and as oppressed and exploited workers.

Michael Joyce, the assistant director of the original Royal Court production believed *The Fool* to be 'Bond's most accessible play since *Saved*';[3] however, Bridget Turner, who played Patty in that production, made some astute comments about Bond's audiences which paint a slightly different picture.

> The audience react in a very strange way to Edward Bond. You feel that very strongly. You get no help from the audience. No feedback in the normal sense. You never feel you're in control of them. It's an odd experience. They don't seem to know how to react to Bond. They seem to be in awe of him.[4]

It may be that the status of being a 'modern classic', which was frequently attributed to Bond at this time, worked to the writer's disadvantage as well as to his advantage. Bridget Turner's impression that the audience members at the Royal Court were 'in awe' of Bond, and that they did not know how to react to him, may well have been a function of that particular production. Even so, it is particularly ironic in the light of his stated aim of engaging the audience as active meaning-makers in the theatrical event. It does reflect a slightly uneasy relationship which has sometimes existed between Bond and the British theatre-going public (Bond's plays have always been more popular in continental Europe than in the UK). It is perhaps because of this that a strand of Bond's theatrical output which took place outside the mainstream theatre was particularly important in his own development as a writer.

OCCASIONAL PLAYS AND TRANSLATIONS

Bond's reputation, inevitably, depends largely upon his full-length plays, those works such as *Saved* and *Lear* which were written for and first staged in the major national producing theatres. However, throughout his career he has also written 'occasional' theatre pieces, responding to a call or a commission for a play for a particular event or occasion, or relating to a specific political issue. These include *Black Mass* (1970), *Passion* (1971), *Stone* (1976), *A-A-America* (1976) and *September* (1989).

Black Mass (1970) was written for the Anti-Apartheid Movement's Tenth Anniversary Commemoration of the Sharpeville Massacre, the mass protest in South Africa which ended in hundreds of deaths and injuries when government troops opened fire on crowds of black men, women and children. Bond's play depicts an avenging Christ who comes down from his cross in the church at Vereeniging to poison the communion wine drunk by the South African prime minister. *Passion: a play for CND* (1971) also draws on and subverts traditional Christian imagery. Here a war memorial in the shape of a crucified pig is unveiled while the Queen and her prime minister simultaneously push the buttons which unleash more and more powerful bombs. Christ and Buddha limp through the ensuing wilderness, on their way to Christ's crucifixion, but the pig has pre-empted them and they turn away in despair. Bond uses these religious images in ways which are designed to shock traditionalists. The scenes of these short plays also contain a comedy which is both broad and savage (in *Passion*, scientists and politicians prove their intelligence and power by their skill at playing with yo-yos). But the seriousness of purpose behind Bond's use of such imagery takes this well beyond parody. An uncompromising atheist, Bond is one of the few late twentieth-century playwrights who can use Christian imagery convincingly.

Several of these occasional pieces have been first staged in non-traditional performance spaces: *Passion* was first shown in an open-air production at Alexandra Park Racecourse as part of the 1971 CND Festival of Life. More recently *September* (1989) was written at the request of the World Wildlife Fund and first performed in Canterbury Cathedral. It, too, lasts about twenty minutes, it is written for a cast of three, and concerns Chico Mendez, the murdered Brazilian leader of the Rural Workers' Union. It is perhaps oversimplifying things to suggest that these short pieces are to Bond what the *Lehrstücke* were to Brecht, but the comparison certainly suggests itself. In terms of the contexts and purposes of their staging, as well as of some of the conventions they draw upon, these plays might be classed as 'agit-prop'. They do not have, however, the didactic simplicity of most agit-prop plays: Bond implicitly mistrusts theatre which preaches to an audience. Nonetheless, the narrative compression of these plays, their tendency to go for the broad effect rather than the subtle one, and their need to speak to what is not necessarily a typically theatregoing audience, all have allowed Bond to explore a very direct and imagistic form of theatre. A particularly powerful example of Bond's work in these occasional plays is *The Swing*, one of the two short plays which make up Bond's *A-A-America* (the title is pronounced like a sneeze!). One of the protagonists, the African-American Paul, describes a historical incident which inspired the action of the play:

> In the fall of nineteen eleven in Livermore Kentucky a blackman was charged with murder. He was taken to the local theatre and tied to a stake on stage. The box office sold tickets accordin' to the usual custom: the more you paid the better you sat. The performance was this: people in the pricey seats got to empty their revolvers into the man. People in the gallery got one shot. An pro rata in between. Course he died very easy compared t' the style of some lynchin's. What you're gonna see is substantially true. We thought it right t'give the plot away. Obviously, if there's gonna be a lynchin you'll sit more comfortable if you know exactly what seat history's sat you on. (*AA* 37)

The rest of the play stages an unexpected version of the action Paul describes, in which the victim of the lynching turns out not to be (as we are led to expect) Paul but his white friend Fred. Fred dies, shot at by an audience, tied to a swing on stage while a clown cavorts around him, giving the scene an even more macabre air by virtue of his attempts at lightheartedness.

The Swing operates more as poetry than as agit-prop, yet its polemical direction is clear. The metaphors it generates are powerful ones and they refer to the theatrical process itself as much as to the injustice of American racism. The theatre in *The Swing* is first bought up by a local businessman to use as a warehouse and then becomes a place of execution. The play insists that theatre is not separate from wider social and economic processes. And as the fictional audience 'kill' Fred, so the real-life audience inevitably finds itself complicit with that act of mob violence, referring back to the historical racist lynching narrated by Paul. At the same time, however, the predominantly white British audience for which the play was first staged finds itself taken off-balance in another way: it finds that a white man, not a black, is the victim. The audience is positioned both as executioner and as victim: it is not always so easy to tell 'what seat history's sat you on'.

Given Bond's left-wing politics, it is not surprising to find him writing occasionally for this kind of politically committed theatre. It is perhaps more of a surprise to find Bond also working in the opera-house. Agit-prop and opera, one might think, inhabit the opposite ends of a theatrical spectrum. The first is low-budget, usually performed free, and often in streets or factories, demonstrations or picket-lines. It is frequently theatrically unsophisticated and always politically engaged, aimed at a typically working-class audience, and more interested in drawing attention to specific social or political issues than in producing fine art. Opera, on the other hand, has come to represent the epitome of theatregoing as an élitist cultural occasion. Expensive to produce and with concomitantly exorbitant ticket prices, operas play to well-dressed, well-heeled, sophisticated audiences who are expected to be theatrically and musically well educated, and who in turn expect high production values, beautiful costumes and elaborate sets. But what both agit-prop and opera offered Bond, in different ways, was a chance to break further away from the conventions and expectations of audiences in mainstream British theatre, and the assumption that what they would be seeing would be a kind of 'well-made-play'.

Bond's collaborations with the European composer Hans Werner Henze have involved two operas, *We Come to the River* (1976) and *The Cat* (1983), and even more unexpectedly a ballet,

41

Orpheus (1979). Of these the most significant is *We Come to the River*. This project began in 1972 when Henze suggested that they should work together on an operatic adaptation of Marlowe's *Edward II*. Bond responded by producing an original libretto, which he revised over the next four years. *We Come to the River* eventually opened at the Royal Opera House, Covent Garden, in 1976. In *We Come to the River*, the European communist composer and the English Marxist librettist created an operatic text which was revolutionary both in form and content. A victorious general becomes conscience-stricken about the sufferings of war victims. Renouncing war, he is declared mad and confined in an asylum, where the Emperor has him blinded, and where he is eventually killed by the other inmates. In some ways the General resembles Bond's Lear, although he has less insight than – and is treated less sympathetically than – Lear. Bond and Henze make it clear that just renouncing violence is not enough: the political message of the end of the play, which puts power into the hands of the masses, is as direct as any agit-prop theatre piece. At the same time, *We Come to the River* transcends many of the conventions of traditional (which is to say, largely nineteenth-century) opera: it is performed on three separate stages, each with its own orchestra. Characters move between these stages, and action frequently takes place on two or more of them either in counterpoint or sometimes even simultaneously. With three different orchestras, three different vocal lines, three different stage areas, and three different dramatic actions, all playing against each other, the audience is frequently faced with the problem of making sense of a huge amount of dramatic 'information'. At its worst, this leads to confusion, as the various elements collapse into a single mass of sound and movement. At its best, however, it allows for subtle and complex playing off of one dramatic element against another, of shifts in focus and mood, of the counterpointing of tragic and comic effects. The subtitle of *We Come to the River* was *Actions for Music in Two Parts and Eleven Scenes* – a title which emphasizes the extent to which the power of the piece derives from the relationships between its fragmentary parts and different elements. This technique of fragmentation and counterpoint was to be something which Bond increasingly used in his playwriting.

As well as his short 'occasional' plays, and his work in music theatre, Bond's other main area of theatre writing (apart from his own full-length works) has been in the field of translation and adaptation of classic playtexts. He has worked on several of these, sometimes in collaboration with his wife, Elisabeth Bond-Pablé, a respected translator in her own right. Bond's version of Chekhov's *Three Sisters* premièred at the Royal Court in April 1967; his translation of Wedekind's *Spring Awakening* was used for the National Theatre's production in 1974; he translated another Wedekind play, *Lulu*, for the Cambridge Theatre Company in 1992. He has also produced his own adaptations of English-language texts, namely two Jacobean dramas Middleton's *A Chaste Maid in Cheapside* (1966) and Webster's *The White Devil* (1976). As mentioned earlier, Bond's adaptation of Brecht's *Roundheads and Peakheads* was undertaken in order to learn about Brechtian technique, and in all probability each of these various translations and adaptations will have had an influence on Bond's own stylistic development.

Since much of Bond's own dramatic output involves critical engagements with existing texts or genres, it is possible to see a continuum between his translations and adaptations and his own 'original' dramatic output, which ranges from the faithful representation of the translation at one extreme, to the deconstructionist reworking at the other. While his work on Chekhov and Wedekind was essentially concerned with producing usable English-language translations of the original texts, he took rather more liberties with *A Chaste Maid in Cheapside*, for which he not only wrote new versions of obscure lines, but also rearranged the end. When offered a 1975 commission to produce a version of Ibsen's *The Master Builder* for American television, he presented the producers with a radically different telling of the tale, in which the central character, Solness, was depicted as much less heroic than in Ibsen's original. The leading actor complained that it would be bad for his image, and the commissioned translation was never produced.

REWRITINGS: *THE WOMAN* AND *THE BUNDLE*

In *Lear* Bond had attempted to reclaim the scope of Shakespearean tragedy for the contemporary theatre; in *The Woman* (1978) he did the same for Greek tragedy. Once more in this play Bond paints on a large canvas, and once more he reshapes a classical model. *The Woman*, which was directed by Bond himself on the new Olivier stage of the National Theatre, is set at the time of the Trojan wars, and in it he draws on a range of classical Greek dramatic and mythological sources – and then leaves them behind. Originally entitled *The Trojan Woman*, the play's primary debt might seem to be to Euripides' *The Trojan Women*; however, the first half of the play, set in and around Troy itself, draws on various tellings and retellings of the Homeric myth, and concentrates on the bickering and the destructive *realpolitik* leading up to the sack of Troy. As with *Lear*, though, Bond eventually produces a version unlike that of any of his predecessors. The second half of the play moves away from its mythological and dramatic sources, and tells a Brechtian parable-like story of what happened to two of the main characters, Hecuba and Ismene, on a small island in the Aegean, in the aftermath of the war at Troy.

The relationship between *The Woman* and Bond's Greek sources, however, involves a different kind of intertextuality from the one which operated in *Lear*, one which allows Bond more freedom in appropriating the characters and situations of classical Greek tragedies. In the first half of the play, a collage of influences and references swirls around Bond's story of Ismene's doomed attempt to bring about a peaceful end to the conflict. Thus, the original Helen of Troy becomes in this retelling a statue of the 'Goddess of Good Fortune' – a transformation which emphasizes the futility of the conflict, especially since few of the protagonists seem to have any literal belief in the supposedly talismanic powers of the object for which they fight. The traditionally scurrilous Thersites (best known to English audiences from Shakespeare's *Troilus and Cressida*) becomes a grave leader of the Greeks; and Odysseus, Menelaus and Agamemnon are ironically conflated in the compound figure of the characteristically named 'Heros'. The particular way in which Bond appropriates the world of Greek mythology undermines the audience's sense that the logic of tragedy is inevitable. The audience for example 'knows' that the Greeks *do* sack Troy, and that the child Astyanax is killed; yet, since so many other things about this fictional world have been changed, this may too. The audience is caught (like many characters in Bond's plays) between two realities – that of the classical tragedies which Bond assumes they will know, and the unsettlingly different world which Bond then creates out of traditional materials, a world in which all sorts of other outcomes are possible.

The play opens with Priam's death. As the war reaches a point of crisis, Heros' wife, Ismene, works together with the widowed Hecuba in order to devise a plan whereby Troy might be spared and the statue returned. But their efforts are rejected, as both sides seem set on confrontation and carnage. The women are imprisoned, Troy is sacked, and Ismene is eventually condemned to death.

In his earlier plays Bond, like many of his male contemporaries, had dealt more assuredly with issues of class exploitation than with those of patriarchy. In *The Woman*, however, there is a new focus on sexual politics. *The Woman* is the first of many of Bond's plays to feature a female central character; more and more frequently, from this point onwards, it is to be a woman who 'bear[s] the major moral and political responsibilities in [his] plays' (*L2* 198): characters such as a Marthe in *Summer*, Rose in *Restoration*, the Woman in *The War Plays*, Agustina in *Human Cannon*, Irene in *Tuesday*. Bond makes it clear that this is a deliberate choice, not one which attempts to annexe a feminist agenda, but which recognizes the importance of feminist analysis.

> I found that in order to deal with the broadest political problems of our time...it was necessary to write female characters. These characters' problems and attitudes made clear the total problems of society and the total problems of our future. There are of course specific feminist political problems – and it may be good tactics to concentrate on these. But I think that women are in particularly opportune situations to understand all our problems. (*L2* 69)

He adds elsewhere that 'so many of my women characters are more politically active and aware than many of my men characters [because]...I find that to consider almost any contemporary political problem from a woman's point of view throws more light on it, radicalizes the problem' (*L2* 196).

In *The Woman*, the familiar 'two-worlds' dichotomy is given a gender inflection: there is an essential opposition between male and female constructions of reality in the play. The male leaders of both the Trojans and the Greeks are aggressive, destructive, exploitative, competitive. It is the women, Ismene and Hecuba, who work for peace through compromise, who show the ability to nurture and to feel compassion for others. It might be thought that such familiar typifications do no more than recycle cultural clichés about masculine and feminine attributes. The play, however, moves beyond this. The women do represent some sort of hope for humanity in the play, but in the first half the intelligent Ismene (in whom that hope seems initially to reside) is seen to be naïve in her appeal to humane values. Like her namesake in Sophocles' *Antigone*, she seeks to compromise and to avert the tragedy, but her actions only lead her into hopeless confrontation with the leaders of her own side, and she is sentenced to be walled up alive as punishment. At the end of the play's first half it seems as if Ismene, like Antigone herself, has sacrificed her own life for her ideals.

As Part 2 opens, however, we discover that she was cunning enough to escape from her living tomb. She has, however, lost her mind, and is living as a recluse with Hecuba in a fishing community on a distant island, where they had been shipwrecked after the fall of Troy. The naïveté of Ismene's earlier actions is given literal embodiment as 'the cleverest woman in the world' is reduced to the status of a child, mothered by Hecuba. Yet the tougher, more cynical Hecuba has her weaknesses too. Having been metaphorically blind, earlier in the play, to the political manoeuvres which destroyed Troy, she has now blinded herself literally, and it is Ismene who acts as her eyes, reporting on the world to her. The image is resonant in terms of classical tragedy, and of course also connects her with Bond's *Lear*. Thus, in the second part of the play Bond provides literal and explicit images of aspects of these characters, which in Part 2 had been left implicit. The two women have found some sort of refuge on this island, where they have lived for twelve years, and they are joined in this by another fugitive, the 'Dark Man', a crippled ex-miner who has run away from the Athenian silver mines. Their apparent safety is shattered, however, when the Greeks, with their leaders Nestor and Heros, arrive once more. They are still searching for the statue of the goddess, which was lost in the same wreck that threw Ismene and Hecuba up on the island. It is clear that if Heros does not find the statue he will destroy the island community. Hecuba tricks him into agreeing to a trial of strength to ensure his position as the recoverer of the statue: he must run a foot race round the island against the crippled miner. Hecuba contrives, by a trick, that the miner should win, and Heros is killed. The Greek soldiers, disheartened, leave in confusion, and while Hecuba dies in the ensuing storm, the islanders, freed from Athenian rule, return to their peaceful lives.

One commonly held critical account of Bond's artistic development asserts that his greatest asset lay in the creative tension which existed in his early plays between a bleakly realistic awareness of the exploitations and oppressions which exist in human societies, and a qualified optimism that these might be combated, that improvement is possible. This some-times leads to the corollary that he lost this creative tension as he became more politicized; that as he himself became more openly Marxist during the seventies, so his plays less critically articulated a naïvely socialist programme. This is the core of William Gaskill's complaint that in Bond's plays after the mid-seventies 'a reach-me-down Marxism is being spelt out'.[5]

It is true that, during this period, Bond's rhetoric when he talks about his own work, leaves little room for political ambiguity. Amongst the 'Poems Stories and Essays for *The Woman*', which are published alongside the text of the play itself in *Plays: Three*, there is a piece called 'Socialist Rhapsody' (the title refers to *The Woman* itself). This begins with the ringingly traditional phrase 'Socialism is a new understanding of the world' and goes on to explore some of the implications of this for his own playwriting.

> ... a writer has to prove each detail of his story – and that is a difficult way to tell it because the point of the story and the reason for telling it are then easily lost. To tell the story well we need to create a 'world poetry' which will express the individual as a force of history – and self-poetry would be a part of this. We would then have a practical vision of socialism ... This play is a story showing in the characters and actions of its protagonists the cause-and-effect of change – especially the stupidity of reaction and the strength of the under-standing that opposes it. It celebrates change and those who make it. This is what makes the play a socialist rhapsody. (P3 269–70)

Paradoxically, this socialist rhapsody was embraced by the theatrical and critical establishment. *The Woman* was the first contemporary play to be staged at the newly opened Olivier stage at the National Theatre, and the same Irving Wardle who had dismissed the first night of *Saved* as 'a systematic degradation of the human animal' was lyrically enthusiastic about this new play – which also, incidentally, contains its share of child-murder and mutilation:

> Bond has now adopted the role of a revolutionary artist... [and has] taken a crowbar to the great Attic Bastille, with the aim of releasing its mighty victims into a new world where they stand some chance of survival if they use their wits. And, as in the case of *Lear*, it is in no way diminished by comparison with its mighty prototype...[6]

But Christopher Innes, in a famous article entitled 'The Political Spectrum of Edward Bond: From Rationalism to Rhapsody', articulates most clearly the charge that Bond's politics are by now becoming a detriment to his playwriting. 'The difficulty', he complains, 'is the cliché nature of Bond's positive programme, which becomes expressed in an easiness of achievement that is dramatically unjustified'.[7] Speaking specifically of *The Woman*, he adds,

> For the crippled slave to win a race against Heros, who is all that his name implies, demands a deliberate mystification of the audience... Nothing we have seen of the Greek soldiers prepares us for an ending in which they are so dispirited by the death of their leader that they simply leave without any acts of revenge... the final positive state of *The Woman* [depicts a] Golden World of peasant innocence that is not only a somewhat impractical alternative to the modern situation but one that had already been dismissed as illusory escapism in *Lear*.[8]

But to read the play in this way is to oversimplify it and to reduce it to a purely naturalistic piece of theatre. This is not how the play works. It is, as Bond calls it, a 'rhapsody'. The word derives not only from Homeric epic (a rhapsody, technically, is an instalment of an epic recited at one sitting) but also contains connotations, derived from music, of emotional overstatement. *The Woman* turns into rhapsodic mode because, as Bond himself recognized in the same essay,

> *The Woman* is one temporary solution to the problem. It ignores facts of the story in order to clarify the story's point and to make clear

48

why the story is being told. The brutality and reaction of our present society will not be defeated by the alliance between one wise woman and one hardened miner. Many things are necessary: organising, thinking, teaching struggle, knocking at doors, waiting in cells, the courage of great moments and the stamina of ordinary endurance. In *The Woman* I ignore many things because I wish to make clear both the point of the story (that history is a moral force, that morality gets its meaning from human beings and that our actions can have morally good results) and my reason for telling it (to celebrate the world and people of which these things are true).   (P3 269–70)

In *The Woman* the mode shifts – or gradually modulates – from one kind of theatre to another. The latter part of the play, with its variation on the hare-and-tortoise story, is a metaphor which points towards the possibility of those 'morally good results', rather than a solemn programme for socialist answers to the problems of *realpolitik*. The defeat of Heros has the ironic self-consciousness of a comedy's happily-ever-after.

The Woman marks the end of another phase of Bond's writing; it is the last of what Bond called his 'problem plays'. This is a phrase which he uses in a not altogether positive tone. 'We mustn't only write problem plays, we must write answer plays', he insisted in a letter to Tony Coult,[9] and he enlarged upon this theme in a public discussion of his work which took place at the Royal Court's Young Peoples' Theatre Festival in 1977.

I'm now going on to a series of plays which I will call 'answer plays' in which I would like to say: 'I have stated the problem as clearly as I can – now let's try and look at what answers are applicable.'[10]

The first of these 'answer plays' opened in the same year as *The Woman*. *The Bundle* was actually staged a few months earlier than *The Woman*, although it had been written later, and it takes Bond's strategy of engagement with previous dramatic texts one stage further. Like *The Woman* and *Lear*, *The Bundle* (1978) also refers to, rewrites and critiques an existing dramatic text: in this case, however, the text is one of Bond's own. *The Bundle* is Bond's second take on *Narrow Road to the Deep North*. Written at a time when his own political analysis was becoming more overt in his playwriting, and when he was feeling an increasing need to write plays which provided answers to some of the questions raised in his earlier writings, *The Bundle* develops further Bond's concept of epic theatre.

The dramatist can help to create a new theatre by the way he writes. He should dramatize not the story but the analysis. He will still have to present the story coherently, just as the painter must achieve a likeness, because that represents the experience, the anecdotal autobiography the audience brings to the theatre. But the scenes will not present the story in the way that is traditionally thought to be satisfying or coherent. In *The Bundle* I tried to find ways of dramatizing the analysis. (*P5* 134)

In the series of plays which ensued, Bond makes much clearer than ever before the nature of the answers which he thinks are available. In *The Bundle*, for example, Bond starts from the same initial image as he had done in *Narrow Road to the Deep North*, that of the abandoned baby by the side of the river, and the appeal to Basho the poet to turn aside from his journey of personal enlightenment in order to save it. A different kind of play grows out of this shared image, however. In *The Bundle*, the abandoned child becomes the central character, Wang. He is saved and brought up by a ferryman, and later sold as a slave to Basho. Politicized by his experiences, he eventually becomes an outlaw, then a guerrilla leader and revolutionary. The end of the play shows the successful outcome of Wang's rebellion – a success achieved only at a price: many friends and family have been lost on the way. The new society is not a Utopia, and still contains its dangers. Nonetheless, there is little ambiguity about the ending: the fight has been won and the victory is to be celebrated. The 'time of great change' which Wang describes holds out a promise that in the future men and women may indeed 'learn how to live and work so that we may be happy and our moral concern for one another is not wasted' (*P5* 137). Thus *The Bundle* dramatizes an analysis which is overtly and optimistically Marxist.

A rational free culture is based either on a classless society or at least on the conscious struggle to remove class structure and the economic, ecological, psychological and political distortions they cause. A writer's work should be part of this struggle. I've always felt that, but now I see more clearly what is involved . . . When I wrote my first plays I was, naturally, conscious of the weight of the problems. Now I've become more conscious of the strength of human beings to provide answers. The answers aren't always light, easy, or even straightforward, but the purpose – a socialist society – is clear.[11]

Bond's commitment to socialist principles had, in fact, been part of his vision from the beginning, although he admitted in an unpublished 1981 interview with Salvatore Maiorana that it took him some time to articulate an analysis of these principles. Of his earliest works he says 'I didn't have the tools, the understanding. I didn't have the analysis then to make those problems clear in political terms'.[12] Bond's plays and other writings from the late seventies onward show that the tools and understanding have been developed, and the commitment to socialism remains unchanged.

The Bundle carries what is perhaps Bond's clearest and most optimistic political message and, despite his comments about the scenes not presenting the story 'in a way which is traditionally thought to be satisfying or coherent', it also has a much more tightly structured narrative than *Narrow Road*. Once more, it is constructed as an episodic series of scenes, and between these a great deal of unstaged action takes place, which the audience has to reconstruct for itself. Bond was particularly concerned, in *The Bundle*, that the audience should understand the rationale for the ordering of these scenes, which he saw as teaching the audience how to respond to and analyse the action of the play. If the choice of a plotline derived from one of his own plays suggests that Bond is carrying on some kind of argument with his earlier self, his dramaturgy in *The Bundle* suggests that he is also engaged in an argument with and about Brechtian theatrical techniques. It was Brecht who first popularized the use of episodic structures in modern theatre, but Bond strongly disagrees with Brecht's suggestion that 'each scene can be complete in itself and that this isolation of scenes can be used to interpret reality' (*P5* 135). This, argues Bond, amounts to an abdication of artistic responsibility. In *The Bundle*, what is important is not simply the scenes themselves and what happens within them, but the way in which they are ordered, and the meaning which this ordering imposes upon the reality of the play. This is why Bond talks about the importance of 'dramatizing the analysis':

> The 'dramatization of the analysis instead of the story' in both the choice and ordering of the scenes and in the incidents dramatically emphasized in the scenes, is a way of reinstating meaning in literature. It may seem cold and abstract but it is not. The analysis

51

can give us the beauty and vitality that once belonged to myth, without its compromises and intellectual reallocation of meaning. It can be the most exciting part of the play... (P5 136)

As an example of what this means in practice, we can take scene 4 – a scene which is easily susceptible to misinterpretation. In this scene, we see Wang, who has been Basho's slave for nine years, just as his time of servitude is coming to an end. Wang rejoices at his impending freedom, while Basho tries to persuade him to stay on voluntarily, as a 'friend'. As this conversation takes place, the two of them come once more upon a baby, abandoned by the river. Basho, seeing this (as he tends to see everything) as a sign from Heaven, tries to manipulate Wang, to trap him into staying. He urges Wang to 'take the child. Live with it in my house', and offers to help the child – but only if Wang himself will stay. And so, like Basho before him, Wang is faced with the chance to save a helpless innocent. The pressure becomes even more intense, for it is implied that the child's mother is the same woman who abandoned Wang himself all those years ago. The baby may be Wang's brother literally as well as figuratively. Wang struggles with his conscience, and finally refuses.

> How many babies are left to die by the river? How many? For how many centuries?... Is this all? One gush of sweetness and I pick up a child? Who picks up all the rest? How can I hold my arms wide enough to hold them all? Feed them? Care for them? All of them... No! (P5 169)

Described in these terms, the scene may seem to condemn Wang. His decision that if he cannot save the whole world he will not attempt to rescue one single child may appear a rather conventional rationalization of what is essentially a selfish act. He may seem to be even more callous than Basho, in a way, for Basho had simply walked away, leaving the baby Wang a chance of survival, whereas the stage directions make it clear that Wang actually picks up the bundle and throws it into the river to drown.

These negative reactions to Wang need not be suppressed – an audience may well be appalled at the decision to let the child die. The notion that Wang may be no better than Basho is certainly offered as a possibility. But it is counteracted and problematized by a number of things: firstly by an audience's understanding that Basho has (at least partially) constructed the moral dilemma in which Wang finds himself, and that the rejection of the child is Wang's only way to escape from Basho's attempts to trap him into servitude once more. The structure of the play also demands that this decision be seen in the light of the events of scene 1. Wang's soliloquy may end with him making the same decision as Basho came to. However the route by which he reaches that decision is more reminiscent of the Ferryman's compassionate speech (which had ended in the Ferryman, against his better judgement, taking up the infant Wang) than of Basho's careless and egotistical rejection. Moreover, as the play develops, we see that this has been a turning point for Wang. It is the moment from which he begins to act in order to improve the world in which he lives.

Equally significant is the theatrical effect of Wang's 'drowning' of the child:

> [stage direction] *As he hurls the child far into the river he holds a corner of the white sheet in his hand and it unravels, catches the wind and falls to hang from his hand.* (P5 169)

On one level it might be said that this, too, at least shows an advance on Basho's way of dealing with the problem in scene 1. Basho had simply walked away whereas Wang, by his action, at least accepts responsibility for the death of the child. But there is more to it than this: the moment is theatrically a more complex one than may first appear. The phrasing of that stage direction gives an indication of the nature of this complexity. In it, Bond refers simultaneously to 'the child' and 'the white sheet'. In the theatre this depends upon an obvious device: there is no baby in the bundle after all. The effect of a baby is created by simply rolling up a sheet to suggest that a child is wrapped up in it. When Wang throws the child away (in production this is usually given maximum dramatic effect by being done directly towards the audience), he does so by holding onto the end of this sheet, so that as it unravels it turns back again into the stage prop which it always was. For an audience, it is no less powerful a moment when we realize that there is no 'real' baby there, since on one level we always knew that. But the trick – which is simultaneously an illusion and a deconstruction of illusion – confronts us once more with the fact that what we are seeing played out in front of us is not reality, but metaphor. The 'baby' is both more and less than an actual child: it is also a powerful image of the difficulty, the impossibility, of doing good in a world which is fundamentally unjust. As Wang says in a later scene, it is a world in which 'We have not yet earned the right to be kind' (P5 194).

It should be stressed that the moment works on a symbolic level only if it has first worked on a naturalistic one. The technique is not a matter of absolving Wang of responsibility by suddenly saying 'it doesn't matter, it's only a trick'. The audience's 'belief' in the reality of Wang's dilemma is essential – and there *is* guilt attached to what he does. What is important is that our response should not stop at the emotional reaction of 'Oh, how terrible'. It is the contextualization, the analysis of the moment which is important.

POLITICAL WORLDS: *THE WORLDS* AND *RESTORATION*

In *The Worlds* (1979) Bond returned to contemporary Britain for his setting and to a kind of social realism for his dramatic language – the first time he had done so since *Saved*. But far from the working-class domesticity of the earlier play, *The Worlds* portrays a highly public environment, and one which was familiar to newspaper-readers in the England of the late seventies. The play deals with contemporary headline material: strikes, terrorism, boardroom in-fighting and industrial unrest. The central character (whom Bond based on Samuel Beckett) is Trench, the managing director of TCC, a successful, though strike-hit, firm. Trench is abducted by terrorists, acting in support of (but independently from) the striking workers of his firm. He is eventually freed unharmed, but in the meantime he has lost control of his company. The first half of the play ends with a surreal scene in which Trench unveils a company portrait (which turns out to be a seaside photographer's prop) and a polite cocktail party ends up in pandemonium. Like *The Woman*, *The Worlds* employs a two-part structure, and we see that in part two Trench has undergone a mental collapse. Like Shakespeare's Timon, Trench retreats from the world, ending up living in the derelict house where he had previously been held captive. Consequently he finds himself involved in a second kidnap attempt by the same terrorists. This, however, is a badly botched one – instead of the new company chairman himself, they have abducted his chauffeur. In the second half of the play, the focus shifts from Trench to Terry, a union militant who is involved in the industrial action at Trench's firm. The strikers are being urged to end the strike in order to save the kidnap victim's life, and Terry argues against this.

The Worlds applies to modern-day Britain some of the questions about direct revolutionary action which are raised in *The Bundle*. Unsurprisingly, given that it opened only two months before a General Election brought Margaret Thatcher to power in May of that year, *The Worlds* was not a popular success. In all probability the play was too firmly lodged in the discourse of current industrial disputes to be heard clearly. It appeared at a time when the political battle lines were being drawn up, and issues such as union militancy, terrorism and industrial action were increasingly being seen in simplified terms of black and white. This, though, is not how *The Worlds* works. Although Bond is clearly contemptuous of the managers and industrialists he portrays, those critics who assumed that therefore he was using the terrorists as his own spokespersons were misreading the play. It is true that the terrorists have many of the best speeches, including Anna's lecture to Trench, from which the play's title is derived:

> Listen. There are two worlds. Most people think they live in one but they live in two. First there's the daily world in which we live. The world of appearance. There's law and order, right and wrong, good manners. How else could we live and work together? But there's also the *real* world. The world of power, machines, buying, selling, working. That world depends on capital: money! Money can do anything. It gives you the power of giants. The real world obeys the law of money. And there's a paradox about this law: whoever owns the money is owned by it... The earth can't hold two worlds anymore. It's too small. So we make the two worlds one. That's all revolution is: making the two worlds one. (P4 75–6)

It is an eloquent, incisive and moving speech. If *The Worlds* were simply a play in which people debated issues, it might be concluded that Anna is right, that the logic lies with her. But, as Bond says, *The Worlds* is actually 'a highly emotional play. I don't like debate plays. My plays are not Shavian. The characters don't actually sit down and debate things'.[13] Nor is Bond interested simply in inverting the current cultural stereotype and presenting Anna as the 'romantic freedom fighter'. Her lines contain truths, but they are dramatically undercut. She speaks them against the farce of the botched kidnapping, and the indifference of Trench, who takes so little notice of what she says that another character has to restate it a few moments later. In the printed text they are ironically foregrounded by being entitled 'A Lecture' in mock-Brechtian style. The two-part structure of *The Worlds* is not the problem/solution structure of *The Woman*, but one in which the apparently straightforward conflicts of the early scenes (terrorists on the one hand, industrialists on the other, strikers caught somewhere between the two) are replayed with farcical variations in the later part of the play. Just as the 'abandoned child' scenes in *The Bundle* make sense only when seen in the context of each other, so the mirror-image kidnappings and industrial crises of *The Worlds* invite the audience to make connections and judgements for themselves. And for all their insight and idealism, Anna and the other terrorists cannot 'make the two worlds one': their gestures are limited and ineffective, they do not have the support of the strikers they claim to be championing, and they are as isolated within their own rhetoric as the industrialists are in theirs. It is up to people like Terry and the other factory workers to try to bring about change by struggling through the contradictions which the two worlds impose upon them. Thus when, at the end of the play, Terry says 'When they ask me to condemn terror I shall say: no. *You* have no right to ask. You are a terrorist' (*P4* 82), he is not so much endorsing Anna and her companions, as rejecting the terms in which contemporary arguments about terrorism were being couched.

Bond's next play, *Restoration* (1981), continues to explore the theme of the two worlds – transposing it this time to a period setting which enables him to dramatize even more clearly the social distinctions between the different worlds of the master and the servant. In *Restoration*, Bond gestures towards some of the dramatic conventions and stock characters of Restoration comedy. Once more, though, he blurs the specifics of the historical period in which it is set, and of the genre which he seems to be employing. The world of *Restoration* seems to evoke a period just after the Industrial Revolution as much as it does the seventeenth century, and the story itself turns out to be a tragic rather than a comic one. The plot contains two strands, each focusing on a different social group. The 'upper-class' story concerns the impoverished Lord Are, who marries Ann, the daughter of an industrialist, for her considerable wealth. More important, though, is the story of Lord Are's servants. A stereotypical 'good and faithful servant', Bob is presented as gentle, good-natured and conventionally honest: when one of his fellow servants, the town-bred Frank, steals from the Master and Mistress, Bob and his mother, Mrs Hedges, are the first to denounce him. Bob's recently married wife Rose (who is black) sides with Frank and helps him to escape – although the luckless Frank is later recaptured and sentenced to hang. The main action, however, turns on the death of the new Lady Are. She is killed, casually and more or less accidentally, by her husband, who then persuades Bob to take the blame for it. The trusting Bob believes that Are will secure him a pardon, which the aristocrat has no intention of doing. Despite Rose's attempts to save him, Bob goes to the gallows along with Frank.

Bond uses music particularly well in *Restoration*. This may owe something to his collaborations with Hans Werner Henze, but it is also more generally reminiscent of the way in which Brecht used music, not in order to emphasize or elaborate on the spoken dialogue so much as to create a dialectic with it. So in this play, cutting across the Restoration comedy-style scenes are a set of songs, written to be performed in a rock idiom. The contemporary feel of the music is in deliberate contrast with the period setting of the rest of the play, because the function of these songs is to allow some of the characters a language in which they can express a different perspective on their situation. The songs enable characters to step outside the action, but also to step outside their historical moment, and to formulate and articulate insights which would be unavailable to them in their own 'reality'.

Restoration is one of Bond's most effective theatre pieces, complex in structure, operating on a variety of different levels, juxtaposing different theatrical styles, ironically quoting past genres and extraordinarily well controlled in its shifts of pace, tone, emphasis and style. It is also, in conception, as deeply political a play as is *The Worlds*. In a letter printed in the *Guardian* on 31 July 1981 Bond wrote 'I was deeply depressed by the last election and, indeed, I wrote *Restoration* as a consequence. I saw Bob as being the typical, working-class Tory voter, and the play is about his betrayal...So the play couldn't be more topical'.[14] *Restoration* is also the last of Bond's 'answer plays': during the early eighties he began a new phase of exploration.

A SMALLER SCALE: *SUMMER* AND *DEREK*

Restoration talks about the present in terms of the past. Bond's next play has a contemporary setting but its subject matter relates to the past's impact on the present. *Summer* (1982) was another play written for the National Theatre, this time for the smaller Cottesloe stage. It is set on a Mediterranean island in what seems to be the former Yugoslavia, and the story brings together three middle-aged survivors of wartime atrocities on that island. As with *Restoration*, the central theme of the play involves the relationship between a master – or rather, in this case, mistress – and servant. But that relationship here is distanced and problematized. The upper-class Xenia used to be the mistress of the house in which much of the action takes place, but now she lives in London: she is back only as a tourist. The island is no longer half-owned by her family, but is part of a socialist republic, and Marthe, who was once her family's servant, now partially owns the house, although she acts as caretaker and lets out rooms. Xenia's return to the house and the island thus allows her to re-live in some way their former relationship, an attempt which Marthe partially colludes with and partially resists.

Summer also distances, by placing in the past, the incident which overshadows the whole relationship between Marthe and Xenia: during the war Xenia had intervened to save Marthe's life when Marthe was due to be shot by the occupying Germans in retribution for partisan activity. Much of the play revolves around the different meanings which characters attribute to Xenia's action. Xenia herself sees it as an act of individual courage and goodness on her part, for which Marthe should be duly grateful, and she compares it to what she sees as Marthe's treachery and cowardice when, after the war, she had given evidence to the new communist regime against Xenia's father. It is only when Xenia meets an elderly German tourist who had once been part of the occupying force, that she comes to see how another interpretation might be put on her and her family's position. Not realizing to whom he is talking, the German reminisces, telling her with comic clumsiness the story of how a beautiful 'girl in white' had asked the commandant to spare the life of her servant:

> Now parents had begged us for their children on the streets. Tried to climb on the lorries to take their place. We pushed them off. But our commandant gave that servant back to the girl....That girl had a right to ask for anything. We were at war for her...She came from the same class as our officers. She knew that – and what it just meant...She needn't have asked, she could have given an order! (P4 386)

Xenia is shocked into having to confront the notion that her act of 'courage' did not mean what she thought after all. Not only was she in no danger, but the Nazis, for whom the German soldier speaks, regarded her as being on their side. They 'were at war for her', and her action is now re-presented to her, not as a courageous moment of resistance, but as one of collaboration, to which the commandant responded with fraternal courtesy. The meeting with the German, however, leads to no real change for her: he is showing her a picture of herself which she does not want to see, and she turns away from it.

With its cast of only five, *Summer* is almost a chamber piece. It is also strikingly different in style from the work that Bond had been producing during the previous decade, and the confusion which this presented for critics can be heard in their various attempts to locate the play both in the context of Bond's work as a whole and of known theatrical traditions. The theatrical world of *Summer* has been compared to that of Ibsen or Strindberg. Other critics have suggested that 'keeping the Chekhovian influence in mind may help clarify the strategies of *Summer*...(in which) Bond's portraiture directly recalls the class-inflected characters of Chekhov's own plays'.[15] Eva Figes, reviewing the play in the *Times Literary Supplement*, stated confidently that '*Summer* is a modern rendering of *The Tempest*:

the age-old quarrel between the exiled dispossessed Prospero and his kinsman is enacted by Xenia and Martha'.[16] Certainly, as all these comparisons suggest, the smallness of the play's cast size should not be taken to indicate any smallness of intellectual or emotional scale. Paradoxically, though, it is the apparent simplicity of form which Bond employs in *Summer* which makes the play so difficult to contextualize.

Perhaps it is the comparison with Chekhov which is most illuminating. Like Chekhov, Bond compresses large historical and social movements into an apparently mundane middle-class setting. Unlike Chekhov's, though, Bond's plays tend to contain a strong sense of forward movement. In *Summer* much of this movement becomes concentrated into a single stage image. Throughout the play, Marthe has allowed Xenia to continue in the belief that she, Marthe, *does* feel gratitude for Xenia's act of 'bravery' and guilt for her own 'betrayal' of Xenia's father. Finally, on the verge of death, she tells Xenia the truth: that she feels no gratitude, no guilt, that she shares the German soldier's perspective that the Nazis were at war on behalf of people like Xenia's family. Remembering one of her fellow prisoners from the time, an old woman who was *not* saved by Xenia, she recalls that woman's words, 'If I could live to spit in her [Xenia's] face' (*P4* 395). Unexpectedly and violently, Marthe does just that. It is a gesture with which Marthe (now, of course, an old woman herself) forces together the past and the present. With it she seeks to shatter the falsehood maintained over so many years, and, paradoxically, to offer Xenia the understanding which she refused on her encounter with the German tourist. But, once more, Xenia refuses to listen. Trapped by her need to sustain her version of the world, in which she is heroine, not collaborator, she clings tenaciously to her old false beliefs.

Bond did not remain long in this Chekhovian territory (if that is what it was). The style of his next play, *Derek* (1982), is startlingly different once again. *Derek* was written for the Royal Shakespeare Company's Youth Festival in October 1982, and was included in the RSC's touring programme the following year. Lasting only fifty minutes, and once more using a small cast (six, this time), a minimalist set, and only a very few realistic props, it is close in spirit to some of the 'occasional plays' described in the previous chapter. Bond, in fact, describes it as a farce – but then goes on to redefine farce for his own purposes in the 'Author's Note' to the play:

> In conventional farce, reality is not allowed to interfere with the energy of the play. But in this play energy is produced from the reality of the farce. So the play should be performed with farcical energy. But to produce this energy the director and performers must base their work on the realism – social realism – of the play's actions and characters. (*DCAA* 6)

This is a direction which can confuse as much as it clarifies, however, since Bond does not seem to mean what we might expect when he talks about 'social realism'. Certainly the term does not refer simply to the lifelike representation of everyday events and actions. In fact the actual narrative concerns a brain transplant: Derek is a brilliant working-class boy who agrees to swap brains with the upper-class Biff, becomes paralysed, recovers, joins the army and ends up killed in a war, while Biff thrives and prospers as a Member of Parliament. *Derek* echoes *Restoration*'s theme of the exploitation of the poor and gullible by the rich and powerful, and asks questions about the genre of farce in the same way that the earlier play had asked questions about the conventions of Restoration comedy.

BOND AND THE NATIONAL THEATRE

If the early phase of Bond's career had been characterized by his connection with the Royal Court, this next phase brought him into contact with a variety of theatres. He returned to the Court to direct *Restoration*, but *Bingo* opened in Exeter, *After the Assassinations* (1983; unpublished) was staged by and with students at Essex University, *The Bundle* was done by the Royal Shakespeare Company, and *The Woman* and *Summer* were first performed at the National Theatre. Of the National Theatre it was hardly to be expected that a relationship would grow up between the writer and the institution similar to that which had prevailed at the Court: the National had no such tradition of nurturing writers (indeed it has always seemed to adopt a rather anxious attitude towards living writers). Nonetheless, it appeared almost inevitable that a British playwright of Bond's stature should be staged at the National sooner or later, and the

1978 choice of *The Woman* as the first play by a living British writer to be produced on the Olivier stage seemed appropriate.

Bond directed the production himself, but the experience was not a happy one. His time there coincided with a period in that theatre's history when it was particularly crisis-ridden, not least because of its involvement in bitter union disputes. The artistic director, Peter Hall, felt under attack from all sides and was retrenching further and further into an anti-union (and eventually an overtly Thatcherite) position. There was inevitably tension between Hall and Bond, and Hall clearly found both Bond's politics and his personal style difficult to cope with. References scattered through Hall's diary entries for the time give his perspective on the edgy, up-and-down relationship between the two men.

> *Wednesday 22 March*   Most of the afternoon spent with Edward Bond. He is like an engaging boy who has joined a secret gang. In his case the gang is Marxism. He actually asks each of the actors auditioning for his new play what their politics are!...
> *Wednesday 5 April*   Edward Bond and Sebastian Graham-Jones, who is to be his assistant director on *The Woman*, had an enormous row today apparently because Bond attacked Sebastian for going to Harrow...Bond loves confrontation...
> *Wednesday 3 May*   ....A loud and acrimonious session tonight with Edward Bond. We shouted at each other...It was heavy stuff and looks like the beginning of a series of nasty situations...
> *Friday 21 July*   Much of the day watching rehearsals of *The Woman*. The big and pleasurable surprise is that it is magnificently staged. The use Bond has made of the Olivier is exemplary, and the visual emblems are superb. Good meeting with him afterwards: he was open to suggestion; no problem at all.[17]

It is important to note Hall's eventual enthusiasm for Bond's direction of *The Woman*, since it has become the received wisdom that Bond does not direct his own plays well. Simon Callow, who played Lord Are in the original production of *Restoration* which Bond directed on his return to the Royal Court in 1981, says that

> since Gaskill's inspired production of *Saved*, no one has understood the style in which the plays are written – not Gaskill, not Peter Gill, and now, least of all it would seem, Bond himself...Edward has determined that no one should direct his plays in future but himself. He has not felt it necessary, however, to add to his writer's craft any apprehension of the crafts of either the director or the actor.[18]

Hall's enthusiastic description of Bond's production of *The Woman*, however, suggests Callow's remark is far from the whole truth.

In fact, Callow turned out to be wrong, too, about Bond taking over the directing of all his own work. He does sometimes direct his own plays – as he did recently with *In the Company of Men* at the Barbican (1996) – but this has been the exception, not the rule, since he worked with Callow in *Restoration*. It should be stressed, too, that Bond's perceived desire for directorial control does not simply amount to the egotism of the artist. As his remarks and notes about his own productions continually show, his productions are not designed to 'fix' the texts, or to have an authorial last word about them; rather they are continual explorations of what he himself has written, attempts to explore them further in the rehearsal room and on the stage. Directing his own plays has also been a coherent response to the contradictions of trying to stage radical work within an institution which he sees as being essentially reactionary. It is one way of trying to protect and further that work in an environment which can seldom be trusted to respond to the spirit in which it was written, and whose own working practices are at variance with the ways in which his plays work. What is more astonishing, after all – that Bond should be interested in the personal politics of his actors, or Peter Hall's amused disdain that he should be so? That Bond, whose Marxist analysis of the workings of class in English society was common knowledge, should have an argument with his assistant director about the latter's Harrovian background, or that an ex-public schoolboy (who, according to Bond, never understood the play in any case) should have been assigned to the project in the first place?

Bond's disenchantment with the National Theatre reached a terminal stage in the early eighties. He describes his growing alienation from it in an obituary notice which he wrote for Yvonne Bryceland, the South African actress who had played Hecuba in *The Woman*, and who died in 1992.

> I wrote for her a play called *Human Cannon*. She was to act it in the Olivier. For reasons I do not care to give, the plan was dropped. I found that a turning point. It meant that for the time being certain things were not going to be possible in our theatre. My play was not

important – and certainly not good enough for her – but she could have used it to show important things.[19]

When he talks about 'our theatre' Bond means not only the National, but British theatre in general. Nonetheless, it was the National Theatre more than any other which came to symbolize for Bond the moribund, lobotomized nature of the British theatre establishment in the Thatcher and post-Thatcher era. He has not worked there since his production of *Summer* in 1982.

3

Postmodernism and Education

Nothing else has the dignity of a crying child

(C. p.xxxiv)

HUMAN CANNON

The National Theatre cancelled the Bryceland *Human Cannon* project, and Bond has not given permission for it to be professionally produced since, despite requests from both the Royal Shakespeare Company and the National itself (Peter Hall changed his mind and offered Bond the chance to stage it with Vanessa Redgrave in the lead. Bond declined). The play was eventually given its first showing in 1986 by an amateur company, Quantum Theatre, in Manchester.

The central protagonist of *Human Cannon*, the one Bryceland would have played, is Agustina, a Spanish peasant woman. She is based loosely on a historical character who was immortalized by Goya in one of his *Disasters of War* etchings. Bond transposes the story from its nineteenth-century origins to the time of the Spanish Civil War (once more juxtaposing two historical periods for those who know the Goya original) making the enemy against whom Agustina fights the Fascists of Franco's army. Like the historical Agustina, who fired the cannon to defend her city against Napoleon's invaders, Bond's Agustina becomes a hero of the resistance. As the troops occupy the city, she tricks a Fascist soldier into teaching her about firing the cannon he guards, then uses her daughter's sexuality to lure him from his post so that she can fire the gun at the dedication ceremony in the munitions factory, where the Fascist leaders are gathered. As she aims the gun, she narrates, making clear her own analysis of what she is doing.

> A woman with a bucket and a mop is invisible. Today I ply the ancient trades of whoring and cleaning. The soldier follows his ancient callings of fornication and war. Inside his general unveils a plaque to the fallen... What will the soldier do? Run back pulling up his trousers, turn and run up and down between the sheds cursing and roaring like a wounded animal... Soldiers will surround him as he stands there shouting and pointing with his trousers round his ankles. He'll be court-martialled and shot.   (P5 76)

And in a blackly funny ending to the first half, we see the gun fired and the soldier rushing on with his trousers down, reacting just as predicted. And because we have been shown in an earlier scene what happens to guards who desert their post we know that she is right: this pathetic comic figure will indeed be shot.

Agustina is another one of Bond's 'immoral' heroes, doing something apparently reprehensible in itself for the sake of a larger good. For a twentieth-century audience familiar with movies, novels and plays which extol the virtues of anti-Fascist resistance fighters in the Second World War, she is actually much less problematic in this respect than most of Bond's heroes – almost a conventional romantic heroine, in fact. But although her firing of the cannon is the apparent climax of the narrative, it comes only at the end of the first half (much as the fall of Troy was a first-half climax in *The Woman*). The play is about more than the legend of the heroic resistance fighter – indeed, Agustina explicitly rejects the mythologizing of her actions in the play's most Brechtian speech:

> What use is a legend? People hear them and say: they're the big ones, we're ordinary... Don't tell me about legends. The gun was there. My enemies walked in front of it. I fired. It was the most ordinary thing I've ever done. I did it for the same reason I lay the table or sweep the floor. If I'm a legend my life is wasted.   (P5 99)

In any case, by this stage, Agustina has not yet become the 'human cannon' – she has merely fired the gun. In the second half the play continues its action/adventure narrative, but also moves into a different mode. Agustina is involved in more guerrilla fighting and eventually captured after detonating a bomb in the village church. To try to extort a confession from her, the Investigator rounds up ten other women from the village as hostages, threatening to execute them all unless Agustina confesses. The scene depicts the standard Fascist response to resistance in occupied Europe.

It also depicts another engagement between Bond and a theatrical classic. Lope de Vega's drama *Fuenteovejuna* (1612–14) tells the story of a town which rebels against and murders its tyrannical overlord. Even under torture no one will name an individual culprit, repeating only that 'Fuenteovejuna [the name of the town] did it'. Since no one culprit can be identified, the king eventually pardons them all. It is a powerful and inspiring story, but it is hard to watch today without a sense that the play is unduly optimistic and idealistic: these townsfolk would stand little chance against a well-ordered military dictatorship. In *Human Cannon* the women hostages repeat the gesture from de Vega's play. Asked 'who planted the bomb in the church?', each gives the name of their village 'Estarobon' (with, ironically, the exception of Agustina, who replies drily 'I don't know, I wasn't there'). It is a poignant moment of solidarity, but this time it does not result in any escape from the logic of oppression. One of the women gives way, and Agustina is executed, along with one other, chosen at random from the hostages as punishment for their resistance. But before her death Agustina's confrontation with the Investigator turns into a surreal theatrical metaphor. She starts to denounce the Fascists

> When you make us weak you teach us to be strong
> When you use secret police you teach us to be secret...
> When you rob us you teach us to sabotage
> When you exploit us you teach us to strike

(P5 114–15)

As Agustina speaks, her struggles with the women who try to restrain her start as naturalism, but end in metaphor:

> *As* AGUSTINA *strains towards the* INVESTIGATOR, *the* WOMEN *hold her and her feet leave the ground so that her body becomes horizontal. The* WOMEN *stand round her like gunners limbering a gun. She raises her head to shout at the* INVESTIGATOR. *The* WOMEN *exclaim in astonishment.* AGUSTINA RUIZ *has become the Human Cannon.*
>
> AGUSTINA. Destroy them! Their world! Cruel! Pull it down!...Aim

me! Head! Higher! Target! Now! Gun speaks! The bomb –
who put – the church? It speaks! Not Estarobon! Fool! It was
Spain! Spain!

(P5 115)

This brilliant stage image repairs poetically the sense of the
women's unity which had been broken by the collapse of the
'*Fuenteovejuna*' moment, and also goes beyond it, pointing to
something beyond their immediate struggle and situation ('It
was Spain! Spain!'). If the problem with Agustina's status as a
'legend' was that it effectively disempowered people, encoura-
ging them to leave things up to the 'big ones', we see here a
visual statement of the women being empowered by Agustina,
taking over her old function of gunner as she herself becomes
the gun. It is an extraordinary moment, and a good early
example of the principle which Bond developed and theorized
in the early nineteen-nineties: his concept of the 'Theatre
Event', or 'TE'.

Actually, to say that Agustina-as-human-cannon 'is' a TE is
misleading, since 'the TE is not the text but what is done to the
text: the use' (L3 74). Bond does not claim to have invented the
TE as a new dramaturgical technique, so much as to have
discovered it as an informing principle of much great drama of
the past as well as the present: properly staged, the plays of
Shakespeare, Sophocles, Chekhov all contain TEs. But Bond's
concern is to write scenes which lend themselves to 'being TE'd'.
A detailed and complex explanation of the theory of TEs can be
found in Bond's *Notes to The War Plays* (WP 298–343). A briefer
description of the term occurs in one of his letters:

> the strategy of TEs is: we select incidents in the story and open these
> incidents out in such a way that they can't be captured by the story
> but must be examined for themselves in relation to the story: then
> 'reality' may impose its interpretation on the story. Of course I write
> in such a way not merely to make this possible – but to demand it. I
> think TEs should be used to act and direct all plays, however ancient:
> then we can see what they meant for their creators and how they can
> have meaning for us. (L1 43)

The aim is to highlight the significant moment (or moments) in
the scene, and to concentrate on them in such a way that their
meanings resonate throughout the scene and throughout the

play. The effect of this is also to move, in another sense, beyond the moment itself towards an analysis of the social and political contexts in which it takes place, and to engage the audience as co-producers of these meanings. If Bond's plays after *Human Cannon* seem increasingly fragmented in their plots, and less and less concerned with continuous or consistent narrative flow, this is at least in part a consequence of his exploration of the theory of TEs.

FRAGMENTED EPICS: *THE WAR PLAYS* AND *JACKETS*

Red, Black and Ignorant (1984) was written very quickly, in December 1983 and January 1984, for the RSC's 'Thoughtcrimes' season on their small London stage, The Pit in the Barbican Centre, where the play premièred on 19 January 1984. It is written to be played with three or more players and in style it 'is derived from agitprop' (*WP* 343), being reminiscent of some of Bond's occasional pieces and parables such as *Passion* or *Black Mass*. Once again, Bond returns to a minimalist set for his drama, suggesting that 'the play may be performed on a stage that is empty except for one bench' (*WP* 2). This spare setting, however, belies the ambition of the play's imaginative scope. This is indicated more accurately by the language of the play, which combines colloquial speech rhythms and powerful but very direct dramatic verse, such as that which opens the play:

Alone of all creatures we know that we pass between birth and death
And wish to teach each new mind to be as profound as a crystal ocean
through which we may see the ocean bed and from shore to shore.

(*WP* 93)

In *Red, Black and Ignorant* 'a man who has never been born recounts the life he did not lead' (*WP* 343). In the text this character is called the 'Monster', and is the ghost of an unborn child, burned in the womb in a nuclear war. The early scenes are fragmentary, juxtaposing poetry and satire, and touching on several recognizable Bondian themes. In one, for example, the Monster's son hesitates to help a trapped and injured woman on the street because she and he, both on the poverty line, are both after the same job. When the Monster intervenes to rescue

69

her, the scene develops into a *Bundle*-like meditation on the theme that 'In bad times it should be human to do good. But in bad times good cannot be done' (*WP* 25). The events in these scenes are thrown into grotesque relief by the continual presence of the Monster himself, whose 'skin, hair and clothes are charred and singed a uniform black so that he appears as if he might have been carved from a piece of coal' (*WP* 2). He is a constant reminder that these things never happened, that between our world and the world of the play lies the chasm of a nuclear attack.

The final scene introduces a new motif, one to which Bond will return insistently in subsequent plays. The Monster's son becomes a soldier (because the Monster's kindness to the trapped Woman had prevented him from finding work as a civilian) and returns home to his neighbourhood on a murderous mission:

> I'm not ashamed to tell you why I'm here. Every squaddie's been sent back to his own street to shoot one civvie-corpse. He chooses which . . . In the end the army's doing this for the public good. (*WP* 30)

It is a dramatic situation which has its origins in a series of improvisations Bond designed for students with whom he was working at Palermo University. The Son eventually chooses to kill his own father – an act which the dying Monster praises as

> defin[ing] rightly what it is to be human . . .
> My son learned it was better to kill what he loved
> Than that one creature who is sick or lame or old or poor or a
> stranger should sit and stare at an empty world and find no reason
>   why it should suffer

> (*WP* 38)

A few months after the Barbican performance of *Red, Black and Ignorant*, the Midland Arts Centre in Birmingham staged the première of a commissioned play which Bond had been working on at around the same time for Bread and Circus Theatre Company, a small group of ex-student actors. Described as 'a short play in three sections', *The Tin Can People* (1984) is another poetic piece of theatre which, like *Red, Black and Ignorant*, has a post-nuclear-holocaust setting. A community of survivors have been living together, surviving on unsullied food out of tin cans, a stranger enters their midst, bringing hope for the community's future – but also apparently carrying a deadly disease. It was after seeing this production that Bond decided to use these two plays as the basis of a trilogy which became known as *The War Plays* – comprising *Red, Black and Ignorant, The Tin Can People*, and a new play, *Great Peace* (1985).

Great Peace falls into two parts. In the first we see a further use of the Palermo improvisation, as the play opens with a situation which mirrors that of *Red, Black and Ignorant*. A soldier on active service returns to his mother's house. There are severe food shortages and all soldiers have been charged with the duty of killing someone from their own neighbourhood in order to increase the chances of survival of the majority. But there is a small but significant change to this version of the improvisation: in a move which links the imagery of this play to many of Bond's earlier works, the soldier has been ordered to kill a baby. In the responses of the soldiers as they talk among themselves, Bond establishes the logic of a world in which such an order can be given and carried out.

> SON. They won't put up no welcome sign next time we come 'ome.
> CORPORAL. Next time there won't be no 'ome to come 'ome to. You pick the kids so they can cut down on paperwork.
> SOLDIER 2. They dont wanna accept responsibility: we pick an they say it was squaddies on the rampage.
> SOLDIER 3. They'll put a couple of us in the glass'ouse t'prove it.
> SOLDIER 1. Nah, they're stirring up the civvie-shit. They get them against us so's we're trigger 'appy when they give us an order t'corpse 'em.
>
> (*WP* 103)

During rehearsals for the play's 1985 production by the Royal Shakespeare Company at the Barbican, the scenes involving the soldier (scenes 1–8 of *Great Peace*) were referred to by the cast and crew as 'the Greek play', stressing the intensity of action of this early part of the play, and the sense, too, in which the narrative is playing for high tragic stakes. The rest of the 'Greek' section shows the working out of the consequences of this order.

The characters in *Great Peace* are, for the most part, called by their functional names. The soldier is simply called the Son. His mother is called the Woman. She, when she becomes aware of his commission, is initially appalled and rejects him, trying to argue him out of his course of action. His first target is the baby of a local woman whom the Woman child-minds, and the Woman tries desperately to protect it. In fact she is successful: he takes the neighbour's child, but, filled with a kind of remorse, returns it to her. But the result of his act of mercy is that he has no child to show his officers. This puts at risk his mother's own youngest child. Realizing the danger, that the soldiers might come for her baby instead, the Woman desperately tries to get her neighbour's child after all, in order to protect her own. She is too late, however: the neighbour has already taken it to a place of safety. Also, the Woman had misunderstood the danger. Still trapped in the consequences of his own act of mercy, in peril himself of being shot for disobeying orders, the Son smothers the Woman's child – his own brother or sister (it is never made clear which). Scene 7 ends with the Woman's dawning realization that the child she is nursing is dead. The Son's action has proved too much for him to live with, however. In a bitterly ironic final scene of the 'Greek Play', the Son is summarily and casually executed for refusing to obey another order: to pick up an empty cigarette pack which the Corporal has thrown down. The triviality of this, compared with the momentousness of the order which he *did* obey, has a dual effect – simultaneously heroic and bathetic. The Son has changed, and is rebelling finally against the inhumanity of the machine which had caused him to act so callously earlier. It is a futile rebellion in any practical sense – as futile as Lear's attempt to pull down his wall. It is also a moment typical of a Bond play. Something has been learned, a glimpse of humanity is shown, and the possibility of change is offered: but against this plays a sense of just how small and frail and possibly ludicrous this optimism is in a world whose dominant logic is that of the Captain who orders his execution:

> CAPTAIN. Well, it was a useful demonstration for the others.
> And it got rid of a weak element.
> God knows he gave us a warning – shot – his brother or sister was
> it?
> I was on the *qui vive* for the next stage.
> No place for mavericks in the army.

We mustn't lose the benefit of this: every chance to exercise command helps us to be fit for leadership.

(*WP* 150)

While there is no formal act division in *Great Peace*, the 'Greek play' is, effectively, the first act of the play. It could, however, form a separate unit of dramatic action from what follows, as Bond has suggested in a note in which he explains that it 'could be played in its position in the text or separately on its own. Or it could be played after the first play' (*WP* 343). Since its events precede chronologically those of the second play, whatever choices are made in production result in some form of dislocation – either of dramatic time or of the written text itself. To leave open such choices is a tactic very much in keeping with the 'postmodernism' which Bond was beginning to explore at the time: the fragmentation or dislocation of narrative causality is a typically postmodern technique.

Scenes 9 to 20 of *Great Peace* show what happens to the soldier's mother, called simply the Woman, over a period of years starting seventeen years after the soldiers' massacre of the innocents. The war has clearly been a nuclear one, which has devastated the planet; even after all these years little is left but a nightmarish landscape, desolate and hostile. Through this wilderness wanders the now-crazed Woman, pushing a handcart containing a bundle of rags which she now identifies as the dead child. There is something extraordinarily concentrated about this image, something which recalls the irony of *The Pope's Wedding* being presented on the set of *Happy Days*. The landscape is once again, as some critics have pointed out, reminiscent of Beckett's bleak settings, but across it travels a figure just as likely to remind an audience of Mother Courage and her wagon. 'I don't like the Absurdists,' Bond has said, 'I am an optimist. I believe in the survival of mankind. I don't believe in an *Endgame* or *Waiting for Godot'*.[1] In *Great Peace*, this belief in the survival of mankind is explored in a theatrical universe which calls both on Beckett's pessimism and Brecht's socialist optimism, but which eventually settles for neither.

The Woman also carries resonances from Bond's own works: she is the grieving mother from the 'Greek play', of course, but this also links her with the mothers in *Jackets*, or *Derek*. Her designation, 'the Woman', links her with Hecuba from Bond's earlier 'Greek play', as does her function as a survivor of a devastating war; the two-part structure of *Great Peace* is reminiscent too of the structure of *The Woman*. As she travels, the Woman also replays scenes from earlier Bond plays: like Basho, and Wang, she abandons a new-born child, leaving it to die in the wilderness. Even her bundle of rags refers (in quite a complicated way) back to earlier plays. At one point it attains a voice, turning then into a figure like the ghost of the Gravedigger's Boy in *Lear*, and, like the ghost in *Lear*, it is not until the Woman has accepted its death that she herself can die. This rag-child also refers an audience back to *The Bundle* and the stage effects of the unravelling bundle of rags which Wang throws into the river.

The world of the second part of *Great Peace* is one of shifting realities. The Woman's crazed vision gives us no fixed point from which to view the dream-world through which she travels; we 'know' that her child is only a bundle of rags – but then it speaks, and we are momentarily unsure. As the Woman travels, and we travel with her, we begin to realize that for her it is a journey to come to terms with the past which sent her mad, 'an Odyssey, or an imitation of the medieval travelogues of Chaucer, Boccaccio, Cervantes or Dante' (*WP* 351). The reference to Dante is perhaps the most appropriate, for the Woman's wanderings are, like Dante's, a journey through hell. But this is a journey she undertakes without a friendly guide, for 'the people in *Great Peace*...live in hell and you do not have a guide to your own house' (*WP* 351). And so the Woman is trying to find a way out of her madness, and to understand that madness in order to regain her sanity. To do this she has to encounter once more the figures from her past. Some of these (such as Pemberton and the soldiers who served with her Son) are still alive. Most of the others, however, are dead, and so she projects them onto new characters she meets. She encounters a man whom she identifies as her son, although the audience knows that he is dead. Coming across a sick woman in the wilderness she asks

> Did we meet before the war? I knew a woman like you – younger of
> course. She 'ad a kid – she'd be your daughter's age now. They were
> my neighbours. (*WP* 204)

The audience may be seduced for a time into believing that characters from the first part of the play *are* going to be found again (perhaps miraculously resurrected like Ismene in *The Woman*) in the second part, and that some sort of closure or reconciliation will be found with them. Eventually, though, we realize that these 'coincidences' are actually happening only inside her head and that for her there is no closure in reality. In the real world, she cannot go back and make things right with her past. She can do this only in her own mind – and there, it is possible, there might be some healing.

The extent to which the Woman does succeed in coming to terms with the past is left open, and the ending of the play is very ambiguous. Eventually, she comes into contact with a community of survivors. In some ways they resemble those of *The Tin Can People* (who, we learn earlier in *Great Peace*, had all died), but they have moved beyond that community both materially and spiritually. They have begun to rebuild, to use machines again, and they work selflessly for each other, welcoming strangers joyfully into their midst and dedicating themselves to their healing. But the Woman refuses to be 'rescued' by them: despite their entreaties she remains out in the wilderness where eventually she dies. The survivors' community is portrayed as a humane one, but for the Woman it does not represent any escape from the horror of this post-holocaust world. In such a world, communities, as the fate of the Tin Can People reminded us, are fragile things. Nor, for all the optimism of that community, does Bond want the audience to fall into the trap of romanticism about post-nuclear returns to Eden. The sci-fi cliché that a nuclear holocaust may lead to a 'cleansing' of humanity and the hope for a chance to build a better future, to start over again with a clean slate, has no place in *The War Plays*. Nonetheless, it is made clear that there is some optimism in the play's ending: 'In *Great Peace* the people go to hell to take the world out of the hands of Gods and armies and put it into their own. They are our guides to the ruins' (*WP* 352).

Bond's next venture developed some of the stylistic experimentation of *The War Plays*. Both the multi-part structure and the catalytic figure of the returning soldier from *Great Peace* reappear in *Jackets 1 and 2* (1989). The two parts of *Jackets* mirror each other in theme while being radically different from each other in style and setting. *Jackets 1* is another highly intertextual piece, deriving this time from a Japanese Noh play, the 'Village School' scene of *Sugawara* by Takeda Zumo, in which soldiers search for a royal child, whose very existence poses a political threat to the local warlord. *Jackets 1* also has resonances with other texts, such as the search for the royal child in Brecht's *Caucasian Chalk Circle*, or even the biblical and mystery-play story of 'The Massacre of the Innocents'. Most clearly, it refers back to the 'Greek' play of *Great Peace*, as the soldiers are directed to the wrong child. *Jackets 2* also bears many similarities to the first part of *Great Peace*, including similarities of mood and setting. In a war-torn contemporary European country (which bears more than a passing resemblance to Northern Ireland) a soldier returns home to his neighbourhood. He becomes involved in a complex stratagem whereby a man who was once his childhood friend and who is now a resistance fighter is set up to kill him. This, though, is all part of a plot which has been engineered by the soldier's own officers in order to step up the intensity of the conflict, and to give them an excuse to take reprisals. The jacket in this title refers to the misrecognition of the dead soldier's body, due to the jacket he is wearing; this in turn relates to the misrecognition of the royal child in *Jackets 1*.

Like *The War Plays*, *Jackets* presents questions as to its unity. Is it a single play in two parts, or two thematically linked but discrete plays? In its published form (Methuen 1990), the former is implied. On the stage, however, both options have been explored. It was first staged in its entirety by students and staff at Lancaster University; the British professional première however only encompassed *Jackets 2*, which was produced and toured by the Education and Outreach Department of the Haymarket Theatre, Leicester. Bond himself seems to have changed his mind about the importance of the relationship between the two parts of the play. In a letter to John Clemo in 1990, as the play was being re-rehearsed for a production at the Bush Theatre in London, he stated that 'the second half works on its own' (*L1* 49), but in later conversations he has stated that the two parts work best when seen together. It is true that they are quite distinct in narrative terms, and that no knowledge of Part 1 is necessary to understand what is going on in Part 2. Nonetheless, much of the poetic power of Part 2 derives from the resonances set up by Part 1.

These questions about the relationship of the part to the whole should be compared to Bond's earlier comments about the ordering of scenes in, for example, *The Bundle*. There he was concerned (in contrast to Brecht) to argue the importance of the ordering of scenes as an essential part of the way in which the plays dramatize the analysis of their own narratives. In *The War Plays* and *Jackets 1 and 2*, he is ordering his structure more loosely, allowing a less determinate relationship between the various parts. The inevitable implication of such a strategy is that there is no longer a single definitive analysis to be made. The plays themselves exist in different manifestations (as individual texts, as trilogies, as fragments which may go to make up a larger play) rather than as organic unities, and thus generate multiple meanings. This ties in closely with Bond's own developing interest at the time in postmodernist thought, an interest which amounts to a further phase in Bond's development – a postmodernist series of plays. The 1990 Methuen edition of *In the Company of Men, Jackets* and *September* includes a fragmentary essay entitled 'Notes on Post-Modernism', and the volume as a whole is entitled *Two Post-Modern Plays*. In his 'Commentary on *The War Plays*' written in 1991, Bond retrospectively applies the label of postmodernism to that trilogy too, while in a recent interview he has talked about 'my trilogy of postmodern plays – *Jackets, Company* and *Coffee*'.[2]

The distinguishing marks of mainstream postmodernist thought include the beliefs that traditional grand narratives have collapsed; that truths and values have become relative; and that historical progress should no longer be seen in linear terms. Many of Bond's plays appear to sit comfortably with such beliefs – not only plays from this later and self-consciously postmodern phase of his writing, but also ones from earlier points in his career, written before the term itself became fashionable. Certainly, if ludic intertextuality, the plundering of the cultural icons of the past, a non-linear approach to history, and the elision of genres are taken (as they often are) to be essential strategies of the postmodern in literature or drama, then the majority of Bond's plays might well be described as postmodern, at least in tendency.

Characteristically, though, Bond has his own meaning for the term. Speaking of *Two Post-modern Plays*, he says 'I call the book "postmodern" as a challenge to the usual use of these words' (*L1*

144). His theoretical approach to the concept bears little resemblance to the French tradition characterized by writers such as Baudrillard, Lyotard or Derrida. His 'Notes on Post-Modernism' begin

> These notes concern the history and the present state (known as post-modernity) of the relationship between people, technology and authority, and the way in which theatre and other arts are part of that relationship. (*TPMP* 213)

For Bond, the concept of postmodernism is a logical extension of his Marxism. He remains a committed socialist who adheres to a highly theorized Marxist intellectual tradition, and rejects that brand of academic intellectual radicalism which is not also linked to political radicalism. His writing is driven by a sense of social injustice and a belief that the world can be changed for the better, and that if we are fully to claim our own humanity it must be so changed. Thus he has no time for those strands of academic postmodernism which lead towards a despair of any possibility of social change –

> the meaninglessness of post-structuralism – the nihilism of Baudrillard, the desire for schizophrenia of Deleuze, or the vacancy of Derrida (who sees meaning as a journey round and round the prison of the circle's circumference in the hope of finding the circle's centre).[3]

An indication of what Bond *does* see as the uses of postmodernism is given in the following quotations. In his 1991 'Commentary on *The War Plays*', he says

> *The War Plays* make up a haphazard history of theatre. When I could I used dramatic means from the past, the rest I had to invent. Perhaps that is the proper use of post-modernism? Truth has no style, but it does not follow that a random *mélange* produces subliminal or transcendental truths beyond rational analysis. Post-modernism could take away the sacredness of the past and make history useful to us, so that it ceases to be our torment. It could release the dead from their prisons, free us from ghosts... (*WP* 342)

'Tak[ing] away the sacredness of the past and mak[ing] history useful to us, so that it ceases to be our torment' has always been part of Bond's political and theatrical project. Postmodernism has now, apparently, been pressed into the service of that project. This is emphasized in the final two 'Notes on Post-Modernism', in which it is made clear that postmodernism for Bond is a means to an end rather than an end in itself:

> 81. First there was the theatre of people and animals, then of people and gods, then of people and the devil. Now we need the theatre of people and people. It is made possible by the use of interrogation in post-modernity. If we don't realize it, it is because we are as greedy as the man who wanted two graves.
>
> 82. All revolutions are written on the back of a calendar.

> (*TPMP* 244)

TELEVISION PLAYS: *TUESDAY* AND *OLLY'S PRISON*

1993 saw a new departure for Edward Bond, with the broadcast of two plays written specially for television. Bond was not new to screenwriting as such: he had been involved as a writer in the late sixties and early seventies on several projects for the large screen, working on the screenplays for Antonioni's cult sixties movie *Blow-Up*, as well as *Laughter in the Dark*, *Walkabout* and *Nicholas and Alexandra*. One of the less-publicized facts about Bond's writing career is that in 1966 he was nominated for an Academy Award for Best Screenplay (for *Blow-Up*). However, his writing for the cinema is not something which Bond has ever taken very seriously:

> I write films in order to live. I've never worked on a film script that interested me deeply – or if it did, imagined for one moment that one could be allowed to deal with the subject properly. That's why all my serious writing is done for the theatre, and it's never interfered with there.[4]

The last comment may seem rather ironic in the light of Bond's often stormy relationship with theatre directors. The kind of interference which Bond refers to in film-making, however, is a function of the financial and institutional structure of the industry itself, and it means that the writer has very little say in the creative process – much less so than in the theatre.

Television lies somewhere between the two. It offers more scope to the writer than most film work, yet the institutional organization has produced rigid working practices, and a resulting tendency to reduce even the most innovatory work to recognized formulas. The point of view provided by the choice of camera angle manipulates the viewer's response more insistently than anything that happens on stage, and the television director's part in the creation of meaning is thereby greater than his stage counterpart. Moreover, television has an innate tendency to pull towards naturalism; we have already seen that this can produce distortions if it overwhelms the anti-naturalist dimensions of Bond's work. Despite these limitations, television offered Bond a new creative opportunity in the early nineties, and he responded with *Tuesday* and *Olly's Prison*.

Tuesday was commissioned by the BBC Schools Service, to be broadcast in three weekly parts beginning in March 1993, in a slot aimed at 14- to 17-year-olds. The entire action takes place in the bedroom of Irene, a teenage schoolgirl, revising for her exams. Her boyfriend Brian arrives without warning: he is a soldier who has been on active service in the Gulf and who has deserted and is now on the run, haunted by the memory of a small child he saw wandering in no-man's land.

> A child is lifted from its mother – the cord stretches. It walked away. From its father – mother– us. Children are meant to cry for food. The cold. The dark. Alone. For comfort. It walked away. From everyone. We hate and kill. It had had enough. Children have begun to walk away from human beings...I can't forget the child. I went for the wrong walk. I met myself. (*T*. 19)

Her father intervenes, trying to get Brian to give himself up to the authorities, and the play develops into a violent confrontation in which Irene attempts to shoot her father. The eventual arrival of armed police results in the death of Brian.

In some respects this is Bond's most formally conventional play. The fact that it follows the classical unities of time and place, however, only serves to emphasize the unexpected nature of Irene's own development. 'I set the play in one very small room and it all happens in "real time" of one and a half hours. At the end of it you've got to feel that the girl is completely changed, and that her life will be different after that. She has understood things that, at the beginning of the play, she did not understand' (*T*. 56). Irene's attempt to kill her father fails: she pulls the trigger but the soldier's gun is not loaded. Even so the event is momentous. The wish itself is enough to change her life, her reality, as much as if the bullet had killed her father. Brian had had a moment of clarity in his vision of the child which had led him to run away from killing; the gun he carries is not loaded because he would never kill anyone. But just for a moment, Irene is prepared to kill, and pulling the gun on her father actually *gives* her a moment of clarity.

> I understood. There is a right and wrong, some things shouldn't be. It was right. then. To do it. So I did. I pulled the trigger. And there were no bullets – I can't be touched. It's done. Now. Always, It's mine. I understood... it won't be like this all the time. The confusion will come back – it's outside the door! (*T.* 34)

The father/daughter conflict is repeated in Bond's other television work, *Olly's Prison*, which was screened in May 1993, in three one-hour episodes shown on consecutive nights. Each episode revolves around a central moment of violence. In Part 1 this takes the form of a fatal confrontation between a father and a daughter. It is evening, in a suburban flat belonging to Mike, a single parent, and his teenage daughter Sheila. When Sheila comes home and sits down at the table, Mike makes her a cup of tea, places it in front of her, and tries to make conversation: is something wrong? has she had an argument with Frank, her boyfriend? But Sheila does not reply. She simply sits there staring into middle distance while Mike becomes increasingly frustrated and threatened by her silence and passivity, which he sees as a challenge to his authority. Eventually, his frustration turns to anger: he ends up strangling her. In a state of shock, in which he hardly seems to realize what he has done, he settles down in the armchair to sleep.

Thus the first forty minutes of the play are staged entirely in monologue. The tension rises and falls between the two of them: at one moment Mike is shouting uncontrollably at his daughter, ordering her to drink the tea he has made for her, at another he is pleading with her, cajoling her, trying all he can to break down the barriers he himself has helped to erect. In *Olly's Prison* there are echoes both of Bond's *Lear* and of Shakespeare's. Indeed, the initial confrontation between Mike and Sheila becomes, on one level, a murderous variation on the opening of Shakespeare's play, when Lear demands of Cordelia that she demonstrate her love for him and she refuses, saying 'nothing'. Towards the end of the first episode, Mike gives away his flat to Sheila's boyfriend, Frank (who then turns against him), much as Lear had bequeathed his kingdom to his ungrateful daughters and their husbands. Throughout the play, characters carry the weight of the past around with them, just as Bond's Lear carried the ghost of the Gravedigger's Boy. At the very end of the play, the act of blinding is used – in both *Lear* and *King Lear* – as both physical punishment and psychological metaphor.

Mike is one of Bond's searching protagonists. Throughout the rest of the play he, like Lear, is desperately looking for answers to questions – in particular to the questions of violence which he has himself raised. But whereas in *Lear* Bond played to blackly comic effect with the juxtaposition between violence and the mundane reality of everyday life, for Mike in *Olly's Prison* this becomes a central question of his existence. Not just because of the grotesque tragedy which arose out of what was initially an argument over a cup of tea, but because of something else. The second part of the play shows Mike in prison, serving his sentence for killing Sheila. During this time he is visited by his girlfriend Vera, who has decided to stand by him. During these visits Mike repeats several times the phrase 'I forgot'. At first the viewer is baffled as to what he means, but gradually it becomes clearer: he is remembering the morning after the killing, when he woke in the armchair. He went to answer the doorbell (it was Vera calling round), and during those few brief seconds he had *forgotten* that he had killed his daughter. This is one of the central puzzles for Mike: the intertwining of the mundane and the horrific, and the fact that ordinary everyday reality and the consequences of his own violence can coexist so easily with one another that it should be possible for him to *forget* the terrible thing he has done.

The moment of violence in the second part of the play comes as a surprise to the audience. Mike is about halfway through his sentence, while another prisoner is celebrating his impending release. This is a cocky young man called Smiler who is in prison for having gouged out the eye of a friend in a pub brawl. Smiler is bragging about what he intends to do when he gets out in three days' time. Mike, on the other hand, has found no answers to his questions and is in the depths of despair, planning to commit suicide. Somehow he has got hold of a rope, which he fixes up in a boiler-room. Before he hangs himself, however, he decides to relieve himself, so as not to mess his pants with urine if his bladder gives way (again the introduction of the mundane and the trivial into a moment of high dramatic tension). He goes out of the room, leaving the rope dangling. When he returns, Smiler is hanging there dead. Nobody knows why he has killed himself.

Smiler's death is another of those moments in Bond's plays where different kinds of logic compete for attention. Naturalistic logic means that certain questions should be asked – and answered – about his death: why should someone with such apparent reason to celebrate kill himself? what emotional state was he in? was he being threatened? in some kind of trouble? These, the questions of human motivation, are asked in the play by Smiler's mother, Ellen. Visiting the prison, she is allowed to question Mike – whom she regards with hatred, seeing him as the one who should have died in Smiler's place. Mike cannot give her any answers, and her frustration and anger are depicted in a subtly brilliant image into which all her hatred is concentrated. They sit at a table, with the institutional cups of coffee and four lumps of sugar between them.

> You're breathing his air – everything you do now's a swindle. I'll hate you when I'm dying. Look forward to it. No distractions then . . . just you, to hate. Lie in my bed and hate. I'm glad I came. My pulse is hammering away. D'you take sugar? (*Puts the four sugar lumps one by one in her coffee.*) I don't take it. But you're not having it. (*Stirs coffee.*) A little practice in hate. (*Sips.*) (*OP* 40)

The coffee cup becomes the focus of all Ellen's emotions. The pettiness of taking all four sugar lumps for herself seems almost ridiculous. Yet the conversion of the polite gesture of social interaction ('D'you take sugar?') into this 'little practice in hate' sums up perfectly the hellishness of their relationship at this moment. And for the audience and Mike there is a further dimension of which Ellen is unaware: the coffee cup recalls Sheila's cup of tea and the conflict which began it all for Mike.

So many of the characters in this play are building prisons for themselves inside their own heads. This becomes apparent during the third part of the play. Mike's own prison has been his mental isolation as much as the walls of the institution; Sheila's prison had been her silence; Vera creates a prison for herself when she moves into Mike's old flat and tries to make it into a refuge which will allow them to go back to their past lives. The exact nature of Smiler's own prison is never fully explained, but it seems that his suicide was a desperate way out of it. What is made graphically clear at the end of the play is the meaning of the apparently enigmatic title itself, *Olly's Prison*.

Olly appears in the final part of the play. This takes place after Mike's release from prison, which he leaves only to encounter the burning resentment of Sheila's old boyfriend, Frank. Frank has become a policeman, and still blames Mike not only for Sheila's death, but also for what he sees as Mike's attempt to implicate him in it. When Vera's plans for Mike to come back and live with her after his release result in a disastrous failure, Mike ends up instead at Ellen's home, pleading to be taken in: the death of Smiler still haunts him. Also staying with Ellen, however, is a younger one-eyed man. This is Olly – who turns out to be the friend whom Smiler had half-blinded in the pub fight. Frank is still out to destroy Mike, and easily talks Olly into a scheme: that between them they should frame Mike (who is still on parole) for beating up Olly. This will (a) ensure that Mike goes straight back to gaol, probably for ever, and (b) enable Olly to claim money from the Victim Compensation Fund. The arranged beating, which Frank carries out in Ellen's flat, was staged, in the BBC production, with a slow, inexorable rhythm in which the viewer is shown each stage of Olly's maiming in detail; Frank's execution of it is careful and ruthless and he takes a chilling professional pleasure – not in the violence itself but in the thought of the damage it will eventually do to Mike. It is, however, too severe, and as a result Olly loses the sight in his remaining eye. We see him in hospital, blinded, holding an invalid's mug with a plastic spout (again the image of the cup) and feeling with his hand round the edge of the table top as he realizes 'Thass the map a' my world from now on' (*OP* 69). The play ends before we know the outcome of the case against Mike – although we are left with the impression that it is likely to go badly for him.

For Mike there has been some comfort. Amazingly his relationship with Ellen develops from the hatred in which it began into something like love. At the end of the play Mike lies in bed with Ellen, in a rare moment of peace before the police come to re-arrest him. He tries to articulate what he has begun to understand.

> I know some of the answers. Frank murdered your son. And my daughter. He wasn't there when it happened – he didn't have to be. He did it for the same reason he blinded Olly. How can I make anyone understand that, see the connections? They can't. So the suffering goes on. Olly's prison. He'll never get out of it. We're all in it till it's sorted out.   (*OP* 69–70)

What Mike says is not, of course, meant to be understood as *literally* true. It may well seem that, on a psychological level, Mike's 'answers' are no more than evasions, that he is once more doing what Vera had once accused him of: failing to take responsibility for his own actions and projecting his guilt onto Frank. Yet there is more to it than this. In the manner of a classic tragic hero, Mike has been through a great deal of pain and suffering, some of it of his own making, and there seems to be more ahead for him. It is a natural audience reaction to want that to be compensated for in some way – by some insight that he can bring back and share with us, to make it worthwhile. Mike himself claims to have such an insight, and he articulates it in the last words of the play, in terms which are problematic, but also very resonant. Like Irene in *Tuesday*, Mike is only partially able to articulate what it is that he has understood. It may be more fruitful to understand Mike's speech, not as an answer in itself, nor as the articulation of a fully worked out explanation, but as something partial, something which is still working its way towards an understanding of some sense of a pattern which links the different moments of violence, and which is in some way most clearly represented by the corrupt and hate-driven authority-figure of Frank. *Olly's Prison* may be less of an 'answer play' than Mike's final speech may make it seem, and is postmodernist too in this sense. 'Deconstruction', says Bond in 'Notes on the Imagination', 'has shown that there is no "closure" in thought, nowhere meaning may be secured or value confirmed. But value comes from the imagination *because* it cannot be stabilized by closure' (*C.* p. xxvii).

So, is it possible to say just what it is that Mike – that Bond – is pointing towards? What pattern is it that the vicious Frank, the vengeful figure of authority, comes to stand for in Mike's mind? Something more, certainly, than individual evil or psychologically motivated resentment. *Olly's Prison* makes explicit the pattern of relationships which exists between oppressions within the home and oppressions within the state, between the prisons which society builds and those which people build for themselves. It is into this pattern that the acts of violence in Bond's plays relate, and Mike, in 1995, is still trying to come to terms with the kind of insight which Bond articulated in his 'Note on Violence' in 1977.

> Fortunately the causes of human violence can be easily summed up. It occurs in situations of injustice. It is caused not only by physical threats, but even more significantly by threats to human dignity. That is why, in spite of all the physical benefits of affluence, violence flourishes under capitalism... Violence can't be contained by an equal or even greater force of counter-violence; it can't be sublimated in games; it can't be controlled by a drug in the water supply (because this would also remove the creative tensions necessary to any society); it will only stop when we live in a just society in which all people are equal in all significant respects. (*P1* 13–14)

RECENT PLAYS FOR THE THEATRE: *IN THE COMPANY OF MEN, COFFEE,* AND *AT THE INLAND SEA*

At the time of writing, the most recent play of Bond's to have been given a major professional UK production is *In the Company of Men*, which Bond directed himself for the Royal Shakespeare Company at The Pit, in October 1996. The play had been written long before that, however, and had already been produced abroad (in France it was described as the most important play written since the Second World War). It was published by Methuen, in *Two Postmodern Plays*, which also included *Jackets* and *September*, in 1990. With *In the Company of Men* Bond revisits once more the territory of *The Worlds*. Like the earlier play, its scenes take place in the two contrasting settings of, on the one hand, the plush comfort of the offices and the country houses of managing directors, and, on the other, the squalor of a derelict house. Its main plots involve both the boardroom manipulations of takeovers in the arms industry and a quasi-Oedipal struggle between father and son. Here, though, there are no seventies-style Baader-Meinhof terrorists to act as the external threat to the world of corporate capitalism: *In the Company of Men* shows that world tearing itself apart in a spiral of competitive greed and paranoia.

In the middle of this is Leonard, a Hamlet-like figure caught in political power games of rival father-figures. He is the adopted son of the arms-manufacturing magnate Oldfield, and at first has ambitions to play the corporate power game himself, despite Oldfield's attempts to prevent him. Consequently he soon finds himself trapped into becoming a pawn in the take-over schemes of his father's business rival, Hammond – another, even more sinister 'father' figure. Hammond is a food manufacturer who wants to move into the munitions industry because 'once it was guns or butter. Now it has to be both... No government can refuse it: the starving wouldn't let them – and more important, nor will the rich' (*P5* 383). Hammond tricks Leonard into a position where he must either betray Oldfield or face humiliation in front of him. In desperation he plans instead to kill him, at a public demonstration of Oldfield's latest line of rifle. In the event, he does not go through with the murder. He aims the gun, but is interrupted (or comes to his senses – he himself offers contradictory accounts of this) before he can fire it, and Oldfield survives without ever knowing he was in danger. For Leonard, as for Irene in *Tuesday*, the act of holding and aiming the gun becomes as significant as if he had actually pulled the trigger. By 'killing' his father in his mind, he began the process of freeing himself from the structures which were imprisoning him, and did so without the ensuing guilt of an actual murder. There is even a scapegoat who will take the blame – the servant Bartley who sees the danger of the loaded magazine, speaks out to avert it and is unfairly blamed and dismissed by Oldfield for what seems like carelessness.

'Leonard, like all young people, is searching for his humanity', says Bond (*L3* 184) – another in the long line of Bond heroes to be doing so. His search for that humanity leads him to attempt, eventually, to make his peace with Oldfield, to whom he confesses his attempted murder. The scene is both tragic and comic, though. Just as the murder was incomplete, so is its expiation, for at some point during Leonard's long confessional monologue to his father, Oldfield dies. It is unclear what, if anything, of Leonard's speech he has heard, or even if the confession has killed him by bringing on a heart-attack. There is no clear-cut closure to the relationship between Leonard and Oldfield, either in emotional terms or in financial ones: Oldfield dies with the will whereby he reinherits his son unsigned. As Hammond and his henchman Dodds try to manipulate the situation to their own advantage, Leonard plots a final counter-attack. With Bartley's help, he contrives to commit suicide, in such a way as to take Hammond with him. As Leonard dangles from a noose in a derelict basement, and Hammond examines the will he has recovered from the young man's body

> LEONARD's *left hand comes from his pocket, with smooth silent jerks. There is a pistol in the hand . . . The pistol searches till it finds* HAMMOND *and then stops – aimed . . . A shot.* (P5 427)

The audience is, however, denied the grotesque and farcical satisfaction of seeing the villain killed by a shot from a dead man's hand. The shot misses, Leonard fails to kill once more, and Hammond escapes with the will. Despite the victory of Hammond, there is something strangely celebratory about the play. It depicts a world of corruption and a series of uncompleted actions, yet somehow within all this Leonard shows a kind of heroism.

While the action of *In the Company of Men* takes place in a recognizable and realistically portrayed world of high finance and big business, that of *Coffee* (which was published in 1995, and has received, as yet, no professional performance in the UK) takes place in a much less stable theatrical universe. Once more it is a play which fragments its narrative: it is divided into a series of five scenes, all entitled 'The First House', 'The Second House', and so on – with the exception of the central scene, which is called 'The Big Ditch'. The first and final houses, in which the play begins and ends, are briefly sketched environments which allow the spectator touchstones for some kind of recognizable everyday existence, rooms in apartment blocks in an unnamed city or cities. In the first of these 'houses' lives a young man, Nold, who states his ordinariness: 'I got a good job. Tech one day a week. Savin' up. Get married. People get on with me. I get on with them' (C. 2). As with Irene in *Tuesday*, the play opens with Nold studying in his room; in walks an older man, Gregory, an oddly Beckettian figure, who leads Nold without speaking on a journey to an underground hovel in 'a dark opening in a forest'. In this hovel live an old Woman and her Daughter, who is in her late 20s but who has the mental age of a small child (we are reminded, perhaps of Hecuba and Ismene). Both are starving and Nold tries to help them, going back to try to bring them food. But instead he finds himself involved in a civil war. He becomes a soldier in this war – or perhaps it would be more accurate to say that he 'turns into' a soldier, for the play sketches no personal or psychological development to suggest the change. Rather, he shifts from one state to the next: at one moment he is the part-time student, concerned for the Woman and her Daughter; the next moment he is a soldier in an execution squad. The logic of the world of *Coffee* is an ambiguous one, in which at least two realities and time-schemes are involved. Even Bond was unsure how this experiment would work:

> I was not sure how the two halves of *Coffee* would go together. Nor was the director. But oddly, in performance it wasn't a problem. The director approached both halves as if they were in the same world, in the same time (I don't mean simultaneous time, one precedes the other). The two halves seemed to fit together ...[not] for some vague aesthetic reason but because they are the audience's world, I think.[5]

This first part of the play is darkly surreal and unnerving. It poses more questions than it answers: who are these people? what has brought them together? how does the Woman know Gregory, as she seems to? are we in the 'real' world or are the old Woman and her Daughter, living in their hole in the ground, from some kind of postmodernist folktale? The second part contains no such ambiguities: it is set in a real world, albeit in a reality so violent and appalling that we might want to dismiss it as unreal. Nold becomes one of the soldiers; Gregory reappears as their sergeant; the squad talk about their work. This work turns out to be to gun down unarmed prisoners in the ravine behind them.

The play is based on a historical truth, the immensity of whose carnage makes it clear just how restrained Bond's dramatization of it is. The setting is never made explicit (and by implication this might be a scene from any war in recent history), but in fact the actions of Nold and his comrades are based on events in the Ukraine during the Second World War. In September 1941 the Einsatzgruppen unit of the German army of occupation rounded up thousands of Jews from the city of Kiev. They were transported to Babi Yar, where there is a ravine on the outskirts of the city. There they were massacred by machine gun fire. Many who were not killed were simply thrown into the pit of bodies to be buried alive. The Einsatzgruppen's own files contain records of 33,771 people killed on 29th and 30th September alone, including thousands of children. Over the next two years, over a 100,000 civilians would die in the ravine at Babi Yar.

Coffee appears to be an extreme depiction of violence. In fact, given the circumstances which inspired it, what is most remarkable is its restraint. The section in which the soldiers carry out their massacre, 'The Big Ditch', is on one level a comic scene about muddled military bureaucracy, and the making of a pot of coffee. The soldiers are out of ammunition for their machine guns, so they have to shoot the prisoners with rifles. Shooting people one by one, rather than by strafing them with machine-gun fire, makes the killing just a little bit more personal: the men start to notice the kinds of details about the prisoners which they usually miss. Not that this leads them to any compassion: the boys throwing stones in the park in *Saved* have turned into the soldiers mowing down unarmed civilians on a path on a cliff-face. They can see them stumble, and weep and bleed, but, like the south London hooligans, they can still dehumanize their victims, relating to them as spectacle rather than as fellow beings, while on another part of the stage another soldier unconcernedly makes coffee for the execution squad. The execution squad remains a disciplined killing machine. Its technology, however, is below maximum efficiency. Rifles are less effective than machine-guns, and some of the victims on the cliff-face survive. The soldiers have to go down into the ravine to finish them off.

When, at the end of the play, Nold walks out of the war-torn countryside back to the world of the city, all he can say is 'I survived, I survived' (C. 87). In fact he did more than that. Down in the ravine, he met once more with the Woman and her

Daughter, this time as victims of the massacre. But now he cannot see them only as victims: he has to face them as humans. In a gesture which echoes his response in the earlier part of the play, he shares food with them, and from that moment on his own humanity struggles with his dehumanized identity as a soldier. Gregory, the seasoned sergeant, sees what is happening, and as the Daughter plays unknowingly and happily eats the food which Nold has given her, he uses every means at his disposal to win Nold back, to turn him once more into the unquestioning killer. But it is too late. Nold turns the gun instead on his fellow soldiers and walks away from the slaughter, taking the Daughter with him. In the end his action makes little difference to the victims; the Woman, badly wounded, is left to die, and we are told that the Daughter was later caught and shot by the soldiers. Yet Bond imagines a small act of individual courage which in another sense makes *all* the difference. Against all the odds, a soldier affirms his own capacity for humanity within the hellish environment of these killing pits. There is no record that any real-life soldier of the Einsatzgruppen ever performed such an act.

Three of Bond's recent plays take as their starting point the same basic narrative moment: someone is studying in an apparently normal, even peaceful, room, into which comes a character who brings with them the chaos and horror of a wider history. In *Tuesday* that horror was represented by the Gulf war; in *Coffee* it was the ravine at Babi Yar towards which Gregory leads Nold. In *At the Inland Sea* (1996) Bond once more has the holocaust explode, this time into the suburban bedroom of a schoolboy. *At the Inland Sea* was written in response to a request from Big Brum, the Birmingham-based Theatre-in-Education company. The play was taken on tour with accompanying workshops to schools in the West Midlands area in 1995–6. It begins, like *Tuesday*, in a suburban English home where a teenager is doing schoolwork – preparing, in fact, for a history exam. Both these plays were written for young audiences (though neither is any less sophisticated or challenging than any of Bond's other, 'adult' plays) and the image of exam preparation works well as an image of the adolescent's engagement with the demands, compromises and oppressions of authority. It is at this moment of psychological and social pressure that the Boy's world shifts on its axis: from the huddle of bedclothes arises a figure – the familiar Bondian image of a Woman with a baby. As in *Coffee*, these figures link the protagonist – and the audience – back into the nightmare of twentieth-century history, for this Woman and her child turn out to be victims of the concentration camps. The Woman demands, impossibly, that the Boy should do something to save her child from the holocaust: she asks him to tell a story, the one story that will save the child's life.

> Tell me a story. Then my baby will live (*The Boy reads*) You ask me 'what story?' Tell me! You say 'I have to study my book'. Tell me! You say 'will it save all the children?' No. You say 'how will it save yours?' (*She looks towards the doors*). When they've taken the bodies out they hose the floor. Then they open the doors and push us in...When we go in through the doors the other mothers will cling to their babies. I won't. I'll put mine down in a corner. That'll be safe. Away from the feet. Your story will be in its head – it'll be too still to die. It goes so still when it listens! (*AIS* 11–12)

The Woman's desperation is infectious, and the Boy is thrown into the search for some way to save the child. He tries to make time stand still, and to carry the child out of the gas chambers. The play, however, does not allow for that kind of magical interference in history: to that extent it is even more uncompromising than *Coffee*. Eventually the Boy must take the baby – and us – back to the gas chambers, where it dies with its mother.

At the Inland Sea uses some of the vocabulary of the folktale, without ever succumbing to the winsomeness, the abstractions or the oversimplifications of that genre. Nonetheless, it does put a terrible twist on the old legend of Scheherazade: the story must be told not merely to postpone one's own death but to save – somehow – the life of another. The play contains, too, a character who looks, at first sight, like a comic version of a witch of a fairytale – an Old Woman with long white hair and a battered straw hat, who laughs outrageously when the Boy describes to her the scenes in the death camps. It turns out, though, that the laughter of the Old Woman arises not from malice but from a kind of universal compassion: the dress she wears beneath her smock contains traces of tales of suffering beyond the Boy's imagination:

I walk among the dead and dying! I wipe tears still wet from the dead faces – with this! I mop blood from wounds. I drag it through the ruins. I wear it next to my skin. I see nothing? (*Laughs.*) Look! (*Points to a stain.*) – tears from an old mother mourning her butchered grandchildren. Here's a woman driven mad with suffering – she ripped it with her teeth. This is of chips of flesh from a slaughter pit . . . This is special, this bit: soot from the city that burned black one morning. You saw a room of dying people? (*Laughs.*) I see more pain in the cracked face of a doll than you see in your baby!   (*AIS* 26)

Like the Woman with her baby, this Old Woman comes from a different time, a different reality. 'I'm not yet born,' she tells the Boy. 'One day I will be. One day I'll live on this earth' (*AIS* 30). It is this perspective on universal suffering which prompts the Boy to take the child back to its mother to die. In doing this, however, the Boy is not being pessimistic, but is recognizing that to change the past is not the point. The real question is what to do about the present. He begins to find his story to tell.

The play ends on a note of creative tension. The Boy's own Mother has already made all the compromises with the everyday world: her world is circumscribed by unrewarding work for little pay, and her strongest desire is that her son should do well at school in order to better himself. As the Boy goes through the trauma of his experience, his Mother becomes increasingly agitated. Trapped in the world of common sense, she is unable to see the Woman at first; all she can see is her son being made ill by the stress of exams. There is an ironic contrast here between this contemporary Boy's Mother and the desperate Woman trying to save her child from the death camps. It is true that the Boy's Mother is not a simple authority-figure (like, say, the Father in *Tuesday*), and she too is eventually given a glimpse of the world which the Boy's imagination has summoned up. Nonetheless, at the end of the play – having shared in some of the Boy's experiences – she seems to have reverted to her authority-function, trotting out almost automatically the clichés of parenthood ('While you're under my roof you live by the rules . . . It's for your own good', (*AIS* 34)). She seems almost oblivious as the Boy starts to tell his story, she interrupts him and does not hear the end of it. But perhaps there *is* no end as yet – or if there is, it is for him to tell to someone else. The final moment of the play has the Boy saying to his mother 'I made some tea'. It is another of those small dramatic gestures on which, in Bond's plays, so much can sometimes depend: we are reminded, perhaps, of the way in which cups of tea and coffee have been used to carry meaning in preceding plays, and in *Olly's Prison* in particular. In the context of this particular play, though, the making of tea becomes a symbolic act of reparation. When the Woman had first appeared, the Boy had spilled his tea and broken the cup. Now, in doing this small thing for his Mother, he begins to come back to his own world and metaphorically to pick up the pieces. Like the mending of the broken chair in *Saved*, it is a gesture which makes a connection between the biggest philosophical and humanitarian questions and the material details of everyday life.

4

Conclusions?

Being human is not an instinctive thing: it is learned in the psyche's drama . . . The psyche and society are a theatre or they are a prison. At the heart of all democracy is drama. (*T.* 49–50)

Writing a book of this kind about a living, and still very productive, writer has its particular pleasures and problems. One of the problems is that of writing a concluding chapter. This study looks at Bond's plays up to *At the Inland Sea*: yet the next play to appear may throw all of his previous work into a radically new light. So any conclusions need to be acknowledged as even more temporary and provisional than most critical conclusions. With this in mind, I would like to make four main points.

The first is to emphasize the interrelatedness of Bond's plays. The intertextuality of his work goes far beyond the simple fact that he rewrites *Lear*, or even *Narrow Road*. I have tried to suggest in this study how certain themes, images and characters recur throughout Bond's work, so that Scopey turns into Len, Hecuba and Ismene become the Woman and her Daughter in *Coffee*, the image of the threatened child or the child-bundle haunts the plays from *Saved* onwards, the Palermo improvisation is used and re-used in *The War Plays*, and so on. Bond's plays continually reflect each other in their facets, and illuminate each other. It is easy to misread this as narrowness of vision, or as the result of a style that has become mannered, rather than distinctive. But this is to miss the point. Bond's plays comprise in effect one long, and as yet unfinished, poem. It is true that, despite the great variety of theatrical modes, genres and styles which he employs, Bond's plays are, in a sense, all telling the same story. But it is a story so big and so important that it encompasses a multitude of other narratives: it is the story of what it costs to find our humanity.

On this theme – and this is the second point of the conclusion – Bond is a formidable polemicist, but he is also a superb craftsman. He uses the stage, and occasionally the screen, as a complex, focused and immediate form of communication. The sinews of this stagecraft may be seen in some of the key images discussed in previous chapters: in the way that the theatre audience is made to question itself as it is turned into a lynch-mob in *The Swing*; in the juxtaposition of two perspectives on the same social reality in the dual-centred stage of the prize-fight and the literary conversation in *The Fool*; in the direct and emotional aggro-effect of the challenge to the audience posed by Wang's hurling away of the child in *The Bundle*; in the long, silent, domestic scene which ends in the faint optimism of the mended chair at the end of *Saved*; in Lear's wondering gaze at Fontanelle's anatomized body; in the way one reality arises out of another as the Woman rises out of the bedclothes with her child in *At the Inland Sea*; in the focus on everyday objects such as the cups in *Olly's Prison*. It is theatre events like these which lie at the heart of Bond's plays, and which open out the meanings of the plays and their arguments.

The third point is to make a few brief observations concerning Bond's current situation, direction and status as a writer. His interest in educational theatre continues. He has written another TIE play for Big Brum, entitled *Eleven Vests*, and is the patron of the International Centre for Studies in Drama in Education. For the most part, though, he remains withdrawn from the mainstream British theatre. His own recent return to directing, with *In the Company of Men* at the RSC, does not seem likely to be repeated very frequently. Bond's relationship to that mainstream is perhaps symbolized by the production of *Coffee*, which is about to open at the time of writing. It is being staged at the Royal Court – not, though, by the Court's own company, but by a Welsh community theatre group, Rational Theatre. Thus Bond's contact with the major subsidized theatres continues – but it is contact at a distance, mediated through the work of those committed amateurs whose work Bond tends to prefer to that of most British professional companies. A further ironic twist is added by the fact that the restaging of *Coffee* at the Royal

Court took place at a time when the Court was not even in its permanent home in Sloane Square, but was residing temporarily, during lottery-endowed refurbishment, in the West End. Thus *Coffee* became, paradoxically, Bond's first West End transfer!

Bond remains in his self-imposed semi-exile as far as the UK is concerned. Worldwide, however, his work is better known and more frequently performed than ever before. In Tuscany a 'Progetto Bond', an interdisciplinary project in the context of education for peace, is currently being proposed. In Los Angeles a group called 'Tuesday Laboratory' (named after the play *Tuesday*) has been set up to put some of Bond's theatrical ideas into practice. There have been recent revivals of several early works in major theatres in Europe and America, and Bond believes that his new plays are being staged much better in theatres abroad than they have been at home. In particular, Alain Françon's productions of his work in France seem to suggest that some of the necessary energy which was provided by the early symbiotic relationship with the Royal Court may still be available to him.

As regards the future development of Bond's writing: it would be foolish to speculate about this in relationship to a playwright whose entire career has involved innovation and unpredictable changes of direction. He maintains that he is writing better in his exile than ever before,[1] and what can most confidently be stated is that whatever it is that succeeds Bond's 'post-modern' series, it will be something unexpected. In response to a question put to him recently about whether he felt he was embarking on a new series of plays, he replied,

> I think that I am now writing a new 'series'...I don't want to call the series 'problem' or 'answer' plays. Perhaps 'people' plays – but then 'social' plays? Perhaps even 'understanding' plays – but this would just bring out the triviality of the critics... I won't name my new series yet. It is to do with understanding our situation. It's out of this understanding that I remain an optimist. It depends, I suppose, on how you understand optimism.[2]

This brings me to the final part of the conclusion – which relates to the particular pleasures of writing about a living author. One of these has been the opportunity to ask questions such as 'do you feel you are embarking on a new series of plays?', and have them answered. Edward Bond looked at a late draft of the manuscript of this book, and among some of the helpful comments and criticisms he offered was the remark that 'I miss the struggles I've been involved in'. In response to that, I shall conclude with one of Bond's own most recent poems, which articulates his sense of urgency about his own writing. It conveys the nature of those struggles, and suggests what it is that fuels his often-expressed impatience with contemporary theatre.

A Writer's Story

I was born at 8.30 p.m. on Wednesday the 18th July 1934
In a thunderstorm
An hour before her labour began my mother scrubbed the stairs
    to her flat to clean them for the midwife to tread on.
In the district in which my mother lived medical people were
    regarded as agents of authority
I was first bombed when I was five.
The bombing went on till I was eleven
Later the army taught me ten ways to kill my enemy
And the community taught me a hundred ways to kill my
    neighbour
I saw there was no justice between one part of the community
    and another
An injustice is like a pebble dropped in the middle of the ocean
When the ripples reach the shore they have become tidal waves
    that drown cities
Necessity rules our days by the law of cause-and-effect
Those who govern do not know what a person is
And the governed do not know what a government should be
Instead the evil do evil and because there is no justice the good
    must also do evil
How else can they govern the prison they live in?
I walked the streets and raged
I wanted the stones in the military cemetery to weep for the dead
    beneath them
I wanted the skull to dream of justice
And then I remembered the iron kite that flies in the child's mind
And saw the old touch their white hairs as gently as a sparrow
    nests on the side of an ice-berg
So at twenty I wrote a play
The law of plays must be cause-and-use
To break necessity and show how there may be justice

Like all who lived at the midpoint of this century or were born
    later
I am a citizen of Auschwitz and a citizen of Hiroshima
Of the place where the evil did evil and the place where the good
    did evil
Till there is justice there are no other places on earth
There are only these two places
But I am also a citizen of the just world still to be made[3]

Notes

INTRODUCTION

1. Malcolm Hay and Philip Roberts, *Edward Bond, a companion to the plays* (London: TQ Publications, 1978), 74.
2. 'Modern and Postmodern Theatres', Edward Bond in interview with Ulrich Köppen, *New Theatre Quarterly*, 50 (1997), 104.

CHAPTER 1. FROM THE EARLY PLAYS TO *THE SEA*

1. 'Modern and Postmodern Theatres', Edward Bond in interview with Ulrich Köppen, *New Theatre Quarterly*, 50 (1997), 104.
2. Simon Trussler, *Writers and their Work: Edward Bond* (Harlow: Longman, 1976), 26.
3. Malcolm Hay and Philip Roberts, *Edward Bond, a companion to the plays* (London: TQ Publications, 1978), 8.
4. 'Drama and the Dialectics of Violence' Edward Bond in interview with the editors, *Theatre Quarterly*, 5 (1972), 7.
5. Trussler, *Edward Bond*, 34.
6. *Daily Mail*, 10 December 1962.
7. *Observer*, 16 December 1962.
8. Malcolm Hay and Philip Roberts, *Bond, a study of his plays* (London: Eyre Methuen, 1980), 24.
9. Hay and Roberts, *Bond, a study*, 31.
10. *The Times*, 4 November 1965.
11. *Observer*, 14 November 1966.
12. Philip Roberts (ed.), *Bond on File* (London: Methuen, 1985), 64–5.
13. Roberts, *Bond on File*, 65.
14. Peter Holland, 'Brecht, Bond, Gaskill, and the practice of Political Theatre' (with reply from Edward Bond), *Theatre Quarterly*, 30 (1978), 26.
15. William Gaskill, *A Sense of Direction* (London: Faber and Faber,

1988), 36.
16. 'Drama and the Dialetics of Violence', 8.
17. From the programme of Liverpool Everyman's production of *Lear*, 1975.
18. Roberts, *Bond on File*, 30.
19. *Plays and Players*, July 1973.
20. Letter to the author, May 1997.
21. Gaskill, *A Sense of Direction*, 138.
22. 'Drama and the Dialectics of Violence', 10.

CHAPTER 2. QUESTIONS AND ANSWERS

1. Malcolm Hay and Philip Roberts, *Bond, a study of his plays* (London: Eyre Methuen, 1980), 266.
2. Philip Roberts (ed.), *Bond on File* (London: Methuen, 1985), 33.
3. Walter Donohue, 'Edward Bond's *The Fool* at the Royal Court Theatre', *Theatre Quarterly*, 21 (1976), 21.
4. Donohue, 'Edward Bond's *The Fool*', 16.
5. William Gaskill, *A Sense of Direction* (London: Faber and Faber, 1988), 125.
6. *The Times*, 11 August 1978.
7. Christopher Innes, 'The Political Spectrum of Edward Bond: from Rationalism to Rhapsody', *Modern Drama* XXV, 2 (1982), reprinted in John Russell Brown (ed.) *Modern British Dramatists: New Perspectives* (New Jersey: Prentice-Hall, 1984), 146.
8. Innes, 'The Political Spectrum of Edward Bond', 145–6.
9. Hay and Roberts, *Edward Bond, a companion to the plays* (London: TQ Publications, 1978), 75.
10. Hay and Robers, *Bond, a study*, 266.
11. Malcolm Hay and Philip Roberts, *Edward Bond, a companion*, 75.
12. Roberts, *Bond on File*, 66.
13. Roberts, *Bond on File*, 46–7.
14. Roberts, *Bond on File*, 49.
15. Jenny Spencer, *Dramatic Strategies in the Plays of Edward Bond* (Cambridge: Cambridge University Press, 1992), 205.
16. *The Times Literary Supplement*, 5 February 1982.
17. John Goodwin (ed.), *Peter Hall's Diaries: The Story of a Dramatic Battle* (London: Hamish Hamilton, 1983), 324, 344, 350, 365.
18. Simon Callow, *Being an Actor* (Harmondsworth: Penguin, 1985), 133.
19. *Guardian*, 17 January, 1992.

CHAPTER 3. POSTMODERNISM AND EDUCATION

1. Malcolm Hay and Philip Roberts, *Edward Bond, a companion to the plays* (London: TQ Publications, 1978), 26.
2. 'Modern and Postmodern Theatres', *New Theatre Quarterly*, 50 (1997), 104.
3. Letter to the author, April 1997.
4. Richard Scharine, *The Plays of Edward Bond* (New Jersey and London: Associated University Presses, 1976), 159.
5. Letter to the author, May 1997.

CHAPTER 4. CONCLUSIONS?

1. *Guardian*, 15 October 1992.
2. Letter to the author, April 1997.
3. From the programme of the Rational Theatre production of *Coffee*, 1997.

Select Bibliography

PUBLISHED PLAYS AND POEMS BY EDWARD BOND

A-A-America and *Stone* (London: Methuen, 1976).
Plays One: Saved, Early Morning, The Pope's Wedding (London: Methuen, 1977).
Plays Two: Lear, The Sea, Narrow Road to the Deep North, Black Mass, Passion (London: Methuen, 1978).
Derek and Choruses from After the Assassinations (London: Methuen, 1983).
Plays Three: Bingo, The Fool, The Woman, Stone (London: Methuen, 1987).
Poems 1978–85 (London: Methuen, 1987).
Two Post-Modern Plays: Jackets and In the Company of Men with September (London: Methuen, 1990).
The War Plays (London: Methuen, 1991).
Plays Four: The Worlds, The Activists' Papers, Restoration, Summer (London: Methuen, 1992).
Tuesday (London: Methuen, 1993).
Olly's Prison (London: Methuen, 1993).
Coffee (London: Methuen, 1995).
Plays Five: Human Cannon, The Bundle, Jackets, In the Company of Men (London: Methuen, 1996).
At the Inland Sea (London: Methuen, 1997).

INTERVIEWS, ARTICLES AND LETTERS BY EDWARD BOND

Interview with Giles Gordon, *Transatlantic Review*, 22 (1966), 7–15.
'Thoughts on Contemporary Theatre', discussion with John Willett, Ronald Bryden, Frank Marcus and David Storey, *New Theatre Magazine*, 7:2 (1967).
'A Discussion with Edward Bond', *Gambit*, 17 (1970), 5–38.
'Drama and the Dialectics of Violence', interview with the editors, *Theatre Quarterly*, 5 (1972), 4–14.

Interview with Beverley Matherne and Salvatore Maiorana, *Kansas Quarterly*, 12:4 (1980), 63–72.

Interview with Ian Stuart, *Journal of Dramatic Theory and Criticism*, 8:2 (1994), 129–46.

Ian Stuart (ed.), *Edward Bond Letters I* (Luxembourg: Harwood, 1994).

Interview with Hilde Klein, *Modern Drama*, 38:4 (1995), 408–15.

Ian Stuart (ed.), *Edward Bond Letters II* (Luxembourg: Harwood, 1995).

—— *Edward Bond Letters III* (Luxembourg: Harwood, 1996).

'Modern and Postmodern Theatres', interview with Ulrich Köppen, *New Theatre Quarterly*, 50 (1997), 99–105.

CRITICAL STUDIES

Carpenter, Charles A., 'Bond, Shaffer, Stoppard, Storey: An International Checklist of Commentary', *Modern Drama*, 24 (1981), 546–56. Contains a good bibliography of Bond material from seventies.

Coult, Tony, *The Plays of Edward Bond* (London: Methuen, 1979). Excellent short study of the plays.

Donohue, Walter, 'Edward Bond's *The Fool* at the Royal Court Theatre', *Theatre Quarterly*, 21 (1976). A casebook, with contributions from many involved in the production, including Bond.

Eagleton, Terry, 'Nature and Violence: The Prefaces of Edward Bond' *Critical Quarterly*, 26 (1984), 127–35. An eminent Marxist critical theorist discusses Bond's theory and criticism.

Hay, Malcolm, and Philip Roberts, *Edward Bond, a companion to the plays* (London: TQ Publications, 1978). Contains useful chronology, bibliography and details of the productions of Bond's plays.

—— *Bond, a study of his plays* (London: Eyre Methuen, 1980). Seminal full-length study of Bond's plays from *The Pope's Wedding* to *The Bundle*, making detailed use of unpublished documentary material.

Holland, Peter, 'Brecht, Bond, Gaskill, and the practice of Political Theatre', *Theatre Quarterly*, 30 (1978), 24–35. A study in dramatic influence (with reply from Edward Bond).

Innes, Christopher, 'The Political Spectrum of Edward Bond: from Rationalism to Rhapsody', *Modern Drama* 25:2 (1982), 189–206; reprinted in John Russell Brown (ed.), *Modern British Dramatists: New Perspectives* (New Jersey: Prentice-Hall, 1984), 126–48. Looks at the cycles of Bond's work with a critical eye.

Lappin, Lou, *The Art and Politics of Edward Bond* (New York: Peter Lang, 1987). Analyses Bond's drama in relationship to its politics.

Mathers, Peter, 'Edward Bond directs *Summer* at the Cottesloe, 1982', *New Theatre Quarterly*, 6 (1986).

Reinelt, Janelle, 'Theorizing Utopia: Edward Bond's *War Plays*', in Sue-Ellen Case and Janelle Reinelt (eds), *The Performance of Power: Theatrical Discourse and Politics* (Iowa City: University of Iowa Press, 1991), 221-32. Theorized analysis of *The War Plays*.

Roberts, Philip 'The Search for Epic Drama: Edward Bond's Recent Work', *Modern Drama*, 24 (1981), 458–78. An updating of the Hay and Roberts study (above) to cover *The Worlds, Restoration*, and *Summer*.

Roberts, Philip (ed.), *Bond on File* (London: Methuen, 1985). Extremely valuable collection of resources relating to the plays up to *The Tin Can People*. Includes reviews, excerpts from unpublished letters and interviews, and good synopses of plays.

Scharine, Richard, *The Plays of Edward Bond* (New Jersey and London: Associated University Presses, 1976). Full-length general study of plays.

Spencer, Jenny, *Dramatic Strategies in the Plays of Edward Bond* (Cambridge: Cambridge University Press, 1992). A very insightful and well-theorized study which deals with the 'poetic materialism' of Bond's work up to *The War Plays*.

Stuart, Ian, 'Answering to the Dead: Edward Bond's *Jackets*, 1989–90', *New Theatre Quarterly*, 26 (1991), 171–83. Analysis of the play in production.

—— 'A Political Language for the Theatre: Edward Bond's RSC Workshops, 1992', *New Theatre Quarterly*, 39 (1994), 207–16. An examination of Bond's workshop technique with the RSC.

Trussler, Simon, *Writers and their Work: Edward Bond* (Harlow: Longman, 1976). Short detailed study of early plays.

OTHER BOOKS MENTIONED IN THE TEXT

Callow, Simon, *Being an Actor* (Harmondsworth: Penguin, 1985).

Gaskill, William, *A Sense of Direction* (London: Faber and Faber, 1988).

Goodwin, John (ed.), *Peter Hall's Diaries: The Story of a Dramatic Battle* (London: Hamish Hamilton, 1983).

Index

Absurdism, 8
Alexandra Park, 40
Anti-Apartheid Movement, 39
Antonioni, Michelangelo, 79
Austen, Jane, 24

Babi Yar, 90, 91
Barbican Theatre, viii, 63, 69, 70
Baudrillard, Jean, 78
BBC, viii, 80, 84
Beckett, Samuel, 5, 8, 54, 73, 89
Big Brum Theatre Company, viii,
    91, 96
Bond, Edward
    A-A-America, 39–41
    After the Assassinations, 61
    Asses of Kish, The, 4
    At the Inland Sea, viii, 22, 86,
        91–4, 95, 96
    Bingo, 1, 22, 29–31, 33–5, 36,
        61
    Black Mass, 39, 69
    Blow-Up, vii, 79
    Broken Shepherdess, The, 4
    Bundle, The, vii, 22, 31, 43, 49–
        55, 61, 70, 74, 77, 96
    Cat, The, 41
    Choruses from After the
        Assassinations, 61
    Coffee, viii, 22, 32, 77, 86, 88–
        91,   95, 96
    Derek, viii, 58, 60, 61, 73

Early Morning, vii, 17–19, 20,
    24, 26
Eleven Vests, 96
Fool, The, vii, 1, 31, 33, 35–9, 96
Great Peace, 22, 71–6
Human Cannon, viii, 45, 63–9
In the Company of Men, viii, 63,
    77, 86–8, 96
Jackets, viii, 22, 73, 75–7
Klaxon at Atreus' Palace, 4, 5, 23
Laughter in the Dark, 79
Lear, vii, 23–30, 39, 43, 46, 48,
    74, 81, 82, 95, 96
Narrow Road to the Deep North,
    vii, 17, 19–22, 24, 31, 33, 49,
    50, 95
Nicholas and Alexandra, 79
Olly's Prison, viii, 79, 80–6, 94,
    96
Orpheus, 42
Passion, 39, 40, 69
Performance, The, 4
Pope's Wedding, The, vii, 1, 4,
    5–12, 16, 17, 29, 73
Red, Black and Ignorant, 69–71
Restoration, viii, 32, 45, 54, 56–
    8, 61, 62, 63
Saved, vii, 10–18, 22, 31, 38, 39,
    54, 90, 94, 95, 96
Sea, The, vii, 1, 6, 29, 30
September, 39, 40, 77, 86
Silo's New Ruins, 4

Stone, 39
Summer, viii, 45, 58–60, 61, 64
Swing, The, vii, 40, 41, 96
Tin Can People, The, 70, 71, 75
Tragedy, The, 4
Tuesday, viii, 22, 45, 79–81, 85, 87, 91
Two Post-Modern Plays, 77, 86
Walkabout, 79
War Plays, The, viii, 45, 68–78, 95
We Come to the River, 41, 42
Woman Weeping, A, 4
Woman, The, vii, 1, 22, 33, 36, 43–9, 54, 56, 61–3, 66, 74, 75
Worlds, The, vii, 32, 54–6, 58, 86
Bond-Pablé, Elisabeth, 43
Bread and Circus Theatre Company, 70
Brecht, Bertolt, 5, 20, 21, 22, 40, 43, 44, 51, 56, 73, 77
Brenton, Howard, viii, 5
Bryceland, Yvonne, 63–5
Bush Theatre, London, 76

Callow, Simon, 62, 63
Cambridge Theatre Company, 43
Canterbury Cathedral, 40
Caucasian Chalk Circle, 21, 22, 76
Chekhov, Anton, 43, 59, 60, 68
Clare, John, 35–9
Clemo, John, 76
CND, 39, 40
Coult, Tony, 49
Coventry, vii, 19, 30
Coventry Cathedral, 19

Daily Mail, 6
de Vega, Lope, 67
Deleuze, Gilles, 78
Derrida, Jacques, 78
Devine, George, 31
Einstein, Albert, 20, 26

English Stage Company, 10, 31
Essex University, 61
Esslin, Martin, 29, 30
Euripides, 44

Figes, Eva, 59
Françon, Alain, 97

Gaskill, William, 5, 10, 21, 23, 31, 47
Gill, Peter, 31, 32
Gilliatt, Penelope, 11
Good Person of Szechwan, The, 22
Goya, Francisco de, 65
Graham-Jones, Sebastian, 62
Guardian, The, 58

Hall, Peter, 62, 63, 65
Happy Days, 8, 73
Hare, David, 5
Haymarket Theatre, Leicester, 76
Henze, Hans Werner, 41, 42, 57
Hitler, Adolf, 20, 26

Ibsen, Henrik, 43, 59
Innes, Christopher, 48
International Centre for Studies in Drama in Education, 96

Johnstone, Keith, 8, 23
Joyce, Michael, 38

Lamb, Charles, 36, 37
Lancaster University, 76
Levin, Bernard, 6
Lord Chamberlain, 11, 31
Lyotard, Jean-Francois, 78

Maiorana, Salvatore, 51
Marlowe, Christopher, 42
Marxism, 42, 47, 50, 62, 78
Massacre of the Innocents, The, 76
Mendez, Chico, 40
Middleton, John, 43

Midland Arts Centre, Birmingham, 70

National Theatre, vii, 43, 44, 48, 58, 61–4, 65
Northcott Theatre, Exeter, vii, 29, 31, 61

Observer, 6, 11

Palermo University, 70, 95
People and Cities Conference, 19
Pinter, Harold, 8
Postmodernism, 77–9
'Progetto Bond', 97

Quantum Theatre, Manchester, 65

Rational Theatre, Wales, 32, 96
Redgrave, Vanessa, 65
Royal Court Theatre, vii, 5, 7, 10, 14, 20, 23, 29–32, 37, 43, 49, 61, 96, 97
Royal Opera House, Covent Garden, 42
Royal Shakespeare Company, viii, 21, 60, 65, 69, 86, 96

Rural Workers' Union, 40

Second World War, 66, 90
Shakespeare, William, 23–9, 37, 44, 54, 60, 68, 81, 82
Sharpeville Massacre, 39
Shaw, George Bernard, 56
Sophocles, 46, 48
Spanish Civil War, 65
Stafford-Clark, Max, 32
Strindberg, August, 59
Stuart, Ian, 3

Thatcher, Margaret, 55, 64
'Theatre Event', ('TE'), 68, 69
Times, The, 11
Times Literary Supplement, 59
Trussler, Simon, 1
'Tuesday Laboratory', 97
Turner, Bridget, 38

Verney, Canon Steven, 19

Wardle, Irving, 11, 48
Webster, John, 43
Wedekind, Frank, 43
World Wildlife Fund, 40
Writers' Group, vii, 4, 5, 23, 30, 31

*Recent and
Forthcoming Titles
in the
New Series of*

WRITERS AND
THEIR WORK

*"... this series promises to outshine its own
previously high reputation."*
Times Higher Education Supplement

*"...will build into a fine multi-volume critical
encyclopaedia of English literature."*
Library Review & Reference Review

"...Excellent, informative, readable, and recommended."
NATE News

*"written by outstanding contemporary critics,
whose expertise is flavoured by unashamed enthusiasm for
their subjects and the series' diverse aspirations."*
Times Educational Supplement

*"A useful and timely addition to the ranks of the lit crit and
reviews genre. Written in an accessible and authoritative style."*
Library Association Record

TITLES IN PREPARATION

Title	Author
Chinua Achebe	*Yousef Nahem*
Antony and Cleopatra	*Ken Parker*
Jane Austen	*Meenakshi Mukherjee*
Pat Barker	*Sharon Monteith*
Samuel Beckett	*Keir Elam*
John Betjeman	*Dennis Brown*
William Blake	*John Beer*
Elizabeth Bowen	*Maud Ellmann*
Charlotte Brontë	*Sally Shuttleworth*
Lord Byron	*Drummond Bone*
Daniel Defoe	*Jim Rigney*
Charles Dickens	*Rod Mengham*
Early Modern Sonneteers	*Michael Spiller*
T.S. Eliot	*Colin MacCabe*
Brian Friel	*Geraldine Higgins*
The *Gawain* Poetry	*John Burrow*
The Georgian Poets	*Rennie Parker*
Henry IV	*Peter Bogdanov*
Henry V	*Robert Shaughnessy*
Geoffrey Hill	*Andrew Roberts*
Christopher Isherwood	*Stephen Wade*
Kazuo Ishiguro	*Cynthia Wong*
Ben Jonson	*Anthony Johnson*
John Keats	*Kelvin Everest*
Charles and Mary Lamb	*Michael Baron*
Langland: *Piers Plowman*	*Claire Marshall*
Language Poetry	*Alison Mark*
Macbeth	*Kate McCluskie*
Katherine Mansfield	*Helen Haywood*
Harold Pinter	*Mark Batty*
Alexander Pope	*Pat Rogers*
Dennis Potter	*Derek Paget*
Religious Poets of the 17th Century	*Helen Wilcox*
Revenge Tragedy	*Janet Clare*
Richard III	*Edward Burns*
Siegfried Sassoon	*Jenny Hartley*
Mary Shelley	*Catherine Sharrock*
Stevie Smith	*Alison Light*
Muriel Spark	*Brian Cheyette*
Gertrude Stein	*Nicola Shaughnessy*
Laurence Sterne	*Manfred Pfister*
Tom Stoppard	*Nicholas Cadden*
The Tempest	*Gordon McMullan*
Tennyson	*Seamus Perry*
Derek Walcott	*Stewart Brown*
John Webster	*Thomas Sorge*
Edith Wharton	*Janet Beer*
Women Playwrights of the 1980s	*Dimple Godiwala*
Women Romantic Poets	*Anne Janowitz*
Women Writers of Gothic Literature	*Emma Clery*
Women Writers of the 17th Century	*Ramona Wray*
Women Writers of the Late 19th Century	*Gail Cunningham*

RECENT & FORTHCOMING TITLES

Title	Author
Sylvia Plath	*Elisabeth Bronfen*
Jean Rhys	*Helen Carr*
Richard II	*Margaret Healy*
Dorothy Richardson	*Carol Watts*
John Wilmot, Earl of Rochester	*Germaine Greer*
Romeo and Juliet	*Sasha Roberts*
Christina Rossetti	*Kathryn Burlinson*
Salman Rushdie	*Damian Grant*
Paul Scott	*Jacqueline Banerjee*
The Sensation Novel	*Lyn Pykett*
P.B. Shelley	*Paul Hamilton*
Wole Soyinka	*Mpalive Msiska*
Edmund Spenser	*Colin Burrow*
J.R.R. Tolkien	*Charles Moseley*
Leo Tolstoy	*John Bayley*
Charles Tomlinson	*Tim Clark*
Anthony Trollope	*Andrew Sanders*
Victorian Quest Romance	*Robert Fraser*
Angus Wilson	*Peter Conradi*
Mary Wollstonecraft	*Jane Moore*
Virginia Woolf	*Laura Marcus*
Working Class Fiction	*Ian Haywood*
W.B. Yeats	*Edward Larrissy*
Charlotte Yonge	*Alethea Hayter*

WRITERS AND THEIR WORK
RECENT & FORTHCOMING TITLES

Title	Author
Peter Ackroyd	Susana Onega
Kingsley Amis	Richard Bradford
As You Like It	Penny Gay
W.H. Auden	Stan Smith
Alan Ayckbourn	Michael Holt
J.G. Ballard	Michel Delville
Aphra Behn	Sue Wiseman
Edward Bond	Michael Mangan
Anne Brontë	Betty Jay
Emily Brontë	Stevie Davies
A.S. Byatt	Richard Todd
Caroline Drama	Julie Sanders
Angela Carter	Lorna Sage
Geoffrey Chaucer	Steve Ellis
Children's Literature	Kimberley Reynolds
Caryl Churchill	Elaine Aston
John Clare	John Lucas
S.T. Coleridge	Stephen Bygrave
Joseph Conrad	Cedric Watts
Crime Fiction	Martin Priestman
John Donne	Stevie Davis
Carol Ann Duffy	Deryn Rees Jones
George Eliot	Josephine McDonagh
English Translators of Homer	Simeon Underwood
Henry Fielding	Jenny Uglow
E.M. Forster	Nicholas Royle
Elizabeth Gaskell	Kate Flint
William Golding	Kevin McCarron
Graham Greene	Peter Mudford
Hamlet	Ann Thompson & Neil Taylor
Thomas Hardy	Peter Widdowson
David Hare	Jeremy Ridgman
Tony Harrison	Joe Kelleher
William Hazlitt	J. B. Priestley; R. L. Brett (intro. by Michael Foot)
Seamus Heaney	Andrew Murphy
George Herbert	T.S. Eliot (intro. by Peter Porter)
Henrik Ibsen	Sally Ledger
Henry James – The Later Writing	Barbara Hardy
James Joyce	Steven Connor
Julius Caesar	Mary Hamer
Franz Kafka	Michael Wood
King Lear	Terence Hawkes
Philip Larkin	Laurence Lerner
D.H. Lawrence	Linda Ruth Williams
Doris Lessing	Elizabeth Maslen
C.S. Lewis	William Gray
David Lodge	Bernard Bergonzi
Christopher Marlowe	Thomas Healy
Andrew Marvell	Annabel Patterson
Ian McEwan	Kiernan Ryan
Measure for Measure	Kate Chedgzoy
A Midsummer Night's Dream	Helen Hackett
Vladimir Nabokov	Neil Cornwell
V. S. Naipaul	Suman Gupta
Old English Verse	Graham Holderness
Walter Pater	Laurel Brake
Brian Patten	Linda Cookson

JOHN CLARE
John Lucas

Setting out to recover Clare – whose work was demeaned and damaged by the forces of the literary establishment – as a great poet, John Lucas offers the reader the chance to see the life and work of John Clare, the 'peasant poet' from a new angle. His unique and detailed study portrays a knowing, articulate and radical poet and thinker writing as much out of a tradition of song as of poetry. This is a comprehensive and detailed account of the man and the artist which conveys a strong sense of the writer's social and historical context.

"Clare's unique greatness is asserted and proved in John Lucas's brilliant, sometimes moving, discourse." **Times Educational Supplement.**

John Lucas has written many books on nineteenth- and twentieth-century literature, and is himself a talented poet. He is Professor of English at Loughborough University.

0 7463 0729 2 paperback 96pp

GEORGE HERBERT
T.S. Eliot
With a new introductory essay by **Peter Porter**

Another valuable reissue from the original series, this important study – one of T. S. Eliot's last critical works – examines the writings of George Herbert, considered by Eliot to be one of the loveliest and most profound of English poets. The new essay by well-known poet and critic Peter Porter reassesses Eliot's study, as well as providing a new perspective on Herbert's work. Together, these critical analyses make an invaluable contribution to the available literature on this major English poet.

0 7463 0746 2 paperback 80pp £5.99

CHILDREN'S LITERATURE
Kimberley Reynolds

Children's literature has changed dramatically in the last hundred years and this book identifies and analyses the dominant genres which have evolved during this period. Drawing on a wide range of critical and cultural theories, Kimberley Reynolds looks at children's private reading, examines the relationship between the child reader and the adult writer, and draws some interesting conclusions about children's literature as a forum for shaping the next generation and as a safe place for developing writers' private fantasies.

"The book manages to cover a surprising amount of ground . . . without ever seeming perfunctory. It is a very useful book in an area where a short pithy introduction like this is badly needed." **Times Educational Supplement**

Kimberley Reynolds lectures in English and Women's Studies at Roehampton Institute, where she also runs the Children's Literature Research Unit.

0 7463 0728 4 paperback 112pp

WILLIAM GOLDING
Kevin McCarron

This comprehensive study takes an interdisciplinary approach to the work of William Golding, placing particular emphasis on the anthropological perspective missing from most other texts on his writings. The book covers all his novels, questioning the status of *Lord of the Flies* as his most important work, and giving particular prominence to *The Inheritors*, *Pincher Martin*, *The Spire* and The Sea Trilogy. This in-depth evaluation provides many new insights into the works of one of the twentieth century's greatest writers.

Kevin McCarron is Lecturer in English at Roehampton Institute, where he teaches Modern English and American Literature. He has written widely on the work of William Golding.

0 7463 0735 7 paperback 80pp

WALTER PATER
Laurel Brake

This is the only critical study devoted to the works of Pater, an active participant in the nineteenth-century literary marketplace as an academic, journalist, critic, writer of short stories and novelist. Approaching Pater's writings from the perspective of cultural history, this book covers all his key works, both fiction and non-fiction.

"...grounded in an unmatched scholarly command of Pater's life and writing."
English Association Newsletter

Laurel Brake is Lecturer in Literature at Birkbeck College, University of London, and has written widely on Victorian literature and in particular on Pater.

0 7463 0716 0 paperback 96pp

ANGELA CARTER
Lorna Sage

Angela Carter was probable the most inventive British novelist of her generation. In this fascinating study, Lorna Sage argues that one of the reasons for Carter's enormous success is the extraordinary intelligence with which she read the cultural signs of our times – from structuralism and the study of folk tales in the 1960s – to, more recently, fairy stories and gender politics. The book explores the roots of Carter's originality and covers all her novels, as well as some short stories and non-fiction.

"...this reappraisal of an interesting novelist explores the roots of her originality . . . a useful introduction to the work of Angela Carter.' **Sunday Telegraph**

Lorna Sage teaches at the University of East Anglia, where she is currently Dean of the School of English and American Studies.

0 7463 0727 6 paperback 96pp

IAN McEWAN
Kiernan Ryan

This is the first book-length study of one of the most original and exciting writers to have emerged in Britain in recent years. It provides an introduction to the whole range of McEwan's work, examining his novels, short stories and screenplays in depth and tracing his development from the 'succès de scandale' of *First Love, Last Rites* to the haunting vision of the acclaimed *Black Dogs*.

"(Written with)...conviction and elegance." The Irish Times

Kiernan Ryan is Fellow and Director of Studies in English at New Hall, University of Cambridge.

0 7463 0742 X paperback 80pp

ELIZABETH GASKELL
Kate Flint

Recent critical appraisal has focused on Gaskell both as a novelist of industrial England and on her awareness of the position of women and the problems of the woman writer. Kate Flint reveals how for Gaskell the condition of women was inseparable from broader issues of social change. She shows how recent modes of feminist criticism and theories of narrative work together to illuminate the radicalism and experimentalism which we find in Gaskell's fiction.

Kate Flint is University Lecturer in Victorian and Modern English Literature, and Fellow of Linacre College, Oxford.

0 7463 0718 7 paperback 96pp

KING LEAR
Terence Hawkes

In his concise but thorough analysis of *King Lear* Terence Hawkes offers a full and clear exposition of its complex narrative and thematic structure. By examining the play's central preoccupations and through close analysis of the texture of its verse he seeks to locate it firmly in its own history and the social context to which, clearly, it aims to speak. The result is a challenging critical work which both deepens understanding of this great play and illuminates recent approaches to it.

Terence Hawkes has written several books on both Shakespeare and modern critical theory. He is Professor of English at the University of Wales, Cardiff.

0 7463 0739 X paperback 96pp

JEAN RHYS
Helen Carr

Drawing on her own experience of alienation and conflict as a white-Creole woman, Rhys's novels are recognised as important explorations of gender and colonial power relations. Using feminist and post-colonial theory, Helen Carr's study places Rhys's work in relation to modernist and postmodernist writing and looks closely at how autobiographical material is used by the writer to construct a devastating critique of the greed and cruelty of patriarchy and the Empire.

Helen Carr is Lecturer in English at Goldsmiths College, University of London.

0 7463 0717 9 paperback 96pp

DOROTHY RICHARDSON
Carol Watts

Dorothy Richardson is a major modern novelist whose work is only now beginning to attract the attention of critics, feminists, and cultural theorists. She was one of the earliest novelists to consider the importance of developing a new aesthetic form to represent women's experience and in doing so, she explored many of the new art forms of the twentieth century. Carol Watt's book is an innovative study of her extraordinary thirteen-volume novel, *Pilgrimage* and offers an exciting challenge to the common readings of literary modernism.

Carol Watts is Lecturer in English Literature at Birkbeck College, University of London.

0 7463 0708 X paperback 112pp

APHRA BEHN
Sue Wiseman

Aphra Behn was prolific in all the most commercial genres of her time and wrote widely on many of the most controversial issues of her day – sexual and cultural difference, slavery, politics, and money. Bringing together an analysis of the full range of her writing in poetry, prose and drama, this is the first book-length critical study of Aphra Behn's work, much of which has been hitherto relatively neglected.

Sue Wiseman is Lecturer in English at the University of Warwick.

0 7463 0709 8 paperback 96pp

HENRY JAMES
The Later Writing
Barbara Hardy

Barbara Hardy focuses on Henry James's later works, dating from 1900 to 1916. Offering new readings of the major novels and a re-evaluation of the criticism to date, she considers language and theme in a number of Jamesian works, including *The Ambassadors, The Wings of the Dove* and *The Golden Bowl,* and engages with his autobiographical and travel writing and literary criticism. Hardy's analysis traces two dominant themes – the social construction of character and the nature of creative imagination – and reveals James to be a disturbing analyst of inner life.

Barbara Hardy is Professor Emeritus at Birkbeck College, University of London.

0 7463 0748 9 paperback 96pp

DAVID LODGE
Bernard Bergonzi

Internationally celebrated as both a novelist and a literary critic, David Lodge is one of Britain's most successful and influential living writers. He has been instrumental in introducing and explaining modern literary theory to British readers while maintaining, in regard to his own work, "faith in the future of realistic fiction". Bergonzi's up-to-date and comprehensive study covers both Lodge's critical writing as well as his novels of the past 35 years (from *The Picturegoers* to *Therapy*) and explores how he expresses and convincingly combines metafiction, realism, theology and dazzling comedy.

Bernard Bergonzi is Emeritus Professor of English at the University of Warwick.

0 7463 0755 1 paperback 80pp

DAVID HARE
Jeremy Ridgman

David Hare is one of the most prolific, challenging, and culturally acclaimed playwrights in Britain today. Jeremy Ridgman's study focuses on the dramatic method that drives the complex moral and political narratives of Hare's work. He considers its relationship to its staging and performance, looking in particular at the dramatist's collaborations with director, designer, and performer. Hare's writing for the theatre since 1970 is set alongside his work for television and film and his achievements as director and translator, to provide a detailed insight into key areas of his dramatic technique particularly dialogue, narrative, and epic form.

Jeremy Ridgman is Senior Lecturer in the Department of Drama and Theatre Studies at Roehampton Institute, London

0 7463 0774 8 paperback 96pp

LEO TOLSTOY
John Bayley

Leo Tolstoy's writing remains as lively, as fascinating, and as absorbing as ever and continues to have a profound influence on imaginative writing. This original and elegant study serves as an introduction to Tolstoy, concentrating on his two greatest novels – *War and Peace* and *Anna Karenina* – and the ancillary texts and tales that relate to them. By examining how Tolstoy created a uniquely spacious and complex fictional world, John Bayley provides a fascinating analysis of the novels, explaining why they continue to delight and inform readers today.

John Bayley is Warton Professor of English Emeritus at St Catherine's College, University of Oxford.

0 7463 0744 6 paperback 96pp

EDMUND SPENSER
Colin Burrow

Considered by many to be the greatest Elizabethan poet, Edmund Spenser's writing has inspired both admiration and bewilderment. The grace of Spenser's language and his skilful and enchanting evocation of the fairy world have, for many, been offset by the sheer bulk and complexity of his work. Colin Burrow's considered and highly readable account provides a reading of Spenser which clarifies the genres and conventions used by the writer. Burrow explores the poet's taste for archaism and allegory, his dual attraction to images of vital rebirth and mortal frailty, and his often conflictual relationship with his Queen and with the Irish landscape in which he spent his mature years.

Colin Burrow is Fellow, Tutor and College Lecturer in English at Gonville & Caius College, University of Cambridge.

0 7463 0750 0 paperback 128pp

HENRY FIELDING
Jenny Uglow

In this fresh introduction to his work, Uglow looks at Fielding in his own historical context and in the light of recent critical debates. She identifies and clarifies many of Fielding's central ideas, such as those of judgement, benevolence and mercy which became themes in his novels. Looking not only at the novels, but also at Fielding's drama, essays, journalism and political writings, Uglow traces the author's development, clarifies his ideas on his craft, and provides a fascinating insight into eighteenth-century politics and society.

Jenny Uglow is a critic and publisher.

0 7463 0751 9 paperback 96pp